M000190014

We Want Land to Live

GEOGRAPHIES OF JUSTICE AND SOCIAL TRANSFORMATION

SERIES EDITORS

Nik Heynen, University of Georgia
Mathew Coleman, Ohio State University
Sapana Doshi, University of Arizona

ADVISORY BOARD

Deborah Cowen, University of Toronto
Zeynep Gambetti, Boğaziçi University
Geoff Mann, Simon Fraser University
James McCarthy, Clark University
Beverly Mullings, Queen's University
Harvey Neo, National University of Singapore
Geraldine Pratt, University of British Columbia
Ananya Roy, University of California, Berkeley
Michael Watts, University of California, Berkeley
Ruth Wilson Gilmore, CUNY Graduate Center
Jamie Winders, Syracuse University
Melissa W. Wright, Pennsylvania State University
Brenda S. A. Yeoh, National University of Singapore

We Want Land to Live

MAKING POLITICAL SPACE FOR
FOOD SOVEREIGNTY

AMY TRAUGER

THE UNIVERSITY OF GEORGIA PRESS
Athens

Parts of this book appeared in different form in November 2, 2014, as "Toward a political geography of food sovereignty: Transforming territory, exchange and power in the liberal sovereign state" in *Journal of Peasant Studies* 41(6) and are reprinted by permission of the publisher, Taylor & Francis Ltd., http://www.tandfonline.com.

© 2017 by the University of Georgia Press
Athens, Georgia 30602
www.ugapress.org
All rights reserved
Set in 10/12.5 Minion Pro by Graphic Composition, Inc., Bogart, Georgia

Most University of Georgia Press titles are
available from popular e-book vendors.

Printed digitally

Library of Congress Cataloging-in-Publication Data
Names: Trauger, Amy, author.
Title: We want land to live : making political space for food sovereignty / Amy Trauger.
Description: Athens : University of Georgia Press, [2017] | Series: Geographies of justice and
    social transformation ; 33 | Includes bibliographical references and index.
Identifiers: LCCN 2016025079 | ISBN 9780820350271 (cloth bound : alk. paper) | ISBN
    9780820350288 (pbk. : alk. paper) | ISBN 9780820350264 (e-book)
Subjects: LCSH: Food security. | Food supply. | Agriculture and state. | Land tenure.
Classification: LCC HD9000.5 .T7356 2017 | DDC 338.1/9—dc23 LC record available at
    https://lccn.loc.gov/2016025079

CONTENTS

ILLUSTRATIONS

ACKNOWLEDGMENTS

Writing a book is like taking a long, inspiring journey, and I am grateful to many people for traveling these many miles with me. I would like to thank Don Young, Clyde Yates, and the members of the Athens Permaculture Group, who inspired this journey. I am indebted to Stijn Oosterlynk, Cyrille Cyrano, Monica Truninger, Yve Le Grand, and the Belgium Permaculture Festival organizers for hosting me and educating me about food sovereignty in Europe. I thank Bob Shimek and Winona LaDuke for encouragement and support for the project and Amy Thielen, Aaron Spangler, Becky Thelen, Brad Brunfelt, and my family in Minnesota for helping me out and putting me up. I am grateful to Gail Darrell, Heather Retberg, and Hilda Kurtz for inspiration and support for my work on the Maine food sovereignty ordinances. I am grateful to Amy Ross and the students in our social theory seminar as well as Lowery Parker, Dani Aiello, Mike Krebs, and Catarina Passidomo for helping me think through the many meanings of sovereignty. I am especially grateful to Molly Canfield for letting me turn every conversation about chickens into a conversation about food sovereignty. I thank Jun Borras and anonymous referees from the *Journal of Peasant Studies* who helped strengthen the theoretical backbone of the book. I am also grateful to the participants in the special session on food sovereignty at the 2013 European Society for Rural Sociology annual meeting for helping me think through a more nuanced role for the state in food sovereignty. If I have forgotten anyone, please accept my apologies and my many thanks for your support.

Special thanks to:

Nik Heynen and the rest of the Geographies of Justice and Social Transformation editorial board for your support of the project, as well as Regan Huff, Derek Krissof, Mick Gusinde-Duffy, and the editorial team at the University of Georgia Press for seeing it through.

Bruce Brummit and Cheryl Valois for endless inspiration and food sovereignty writing retreats.

Allison Kennamer and Laura Glenn, who helped me keep body and mind together while writing.

Jennifer Fluri, my favorite political geographer and tireless supporter in all things academic and otherwise.

My mother, who taught me the right way to do things.

Sitara, my star, who fell from the sky into my life as I did the research for this book. You will always be the first and best reason to fight for right.

We Want Land to Live

Political Practice at the Margins

It's Always been a tough row to hoe, an uphill battle, David v Goliath. Bills to *create or preserve or protect legal space* for the direct exchange of food between farmers and customers. . . . The strength [we need] will come from communities as it is now and as it has [been] in the past. We'll need lots of hoes in the garden this session and this town meeting cycle. . . . Reclaiming a voice in the rules governing our food certainly belongs to all of us and the number of voices is only growing. How could we not be optimistic?!

Heather Retberg, personal communication, January 2015, emphasis added

In 2009, state and federal agents seized two hundred gallons of raw milk legally purchased in South Carolina and distributed in Athens, Georgia, from a farmers' market and forced its impoundment and destruction. In 2011, a farmer in Blue Hill, Maine, was arrested for selling raw milk without a license. In 2012, state agents harassed and ticketed a native ricer near the White Earth Indian Reservation in northern Minnesota for having a canoe and a push pole in his truck. In 2013, the city of Lisbon, Portugal, destroyed a community permaculture garden without notifying the gardeners. In 2014, state agents shut down a seed library in Mechanicsburg, Pennsylvania. The list goes on. In the name of food safety, growers and eaters everywhere have been abruptly confronted with legal action and often unlawfully arrested and harassed by state and federal agents of the U.S. Department of Agriculture (USDA) and the Food and Drug Administration (FDA). In a country where discourses of freedom are hegemonic and consumption is deemed patriotic, the right to food is conditioned by what the state and corporations deem to be safe, legal, and profitable and not by what eaters think is right in terms of their own health, the environment, or their communities.

This book is about the David and Goliath struggle that Heather Retberg, a farmer, food sovereignty activist, and representative of Food for Maine's Future references in the opening quote. She speaks directly to the struggle for legal space for small-scale agriculture in Maine through direct local action with ordinances. The Davids in this fight are the small-scale farmers, and the Goliaths are the large corporations and even larger state governments that create and manipulate legislation to further the interests of transnational capital. The winner in so many of these battles so far has *not* been the small-scale producer, for reasons that this book details. These struggles take place all over the world, in backyards, in community gardens, on squatted land, on lakes, in seed banks, and on small-scale farms. This is political practice at the margins, the places often overlooked in search of grander stories or more politically palatable narratives. But the margin always communicates something about the center, perhaps something that those at the center, or those who support the center, choose not to know because it tells them the story of who or what they killed or disempowered to get there.

The meanings of food sovereignty are contested, but at its heart food sovereignty is both a definitional and a material struggle. Food sovereigntists position themselves against the corporate food regime in order to expand the meaning of human rights to include a "Right to Food" as guaranteed by the United Nations Declaration on Human Rights. Food sovereignty confronts what Malik Yakini of the Detroit Black Community Food Security Network calls the "twin evils of white supremacy and capitalism" (2013). It is a struggle that emerges from the margins by and on behalf of the poor, the hungry, and the landless to relocate the spaces of decision making in the global food system. The discursive battleground lies in an ambitious redefinition of the political, the economic, the social, and the ecological in the food system (Nyéléni, 2007). The material struggle for land, food, and seed advances on multiple fronts, mostly on small farms and in local communities and through small but significant acts of defiance, as well as through acts of kindness and love—the "practice of freedom" (hooks, 2006)—made in everyday ways by ordinary people.

Food sovereignty aims to build ecologically based production models, develop postcapitalist politics of exchange, democratize decision making in the food system, and reconnect food producers with food consumers (Nyéléni, 2007; Pimbert, 2009; Wittman, Desmarais, & Wiebe, 2010).[1] While this may seem to resemble what has come before it in the form of organic production, Fair Trade networks, and sustainability-focused social movements, food sovereignty diverges from its many partners and predecessors in significant ways (see also Holt-Giménez & Shattuck, 2011). As stated by a delegate to the 2007 Forum for Food Sovereignty in Mali, food sovereignty means to "exercise autonomy in all *territorial spaces*: countries, regions, cities and rural communities. Food sovereignty is only possible if it takes place at the same time as *political sovereignty* of peoples" (Nyéléni, 2007: 5, emphasis added). Food sovereignty's impact differs because of its overt emphasis on the political economic transformation of communities and territories. It asserts the need for and grapples with the enormous tensions around what Audra Simpson (2014: 10) identifies as the possibility for "sovereignty within sovereignty."

FIGURE 1. Community permaculture garden in a vacant lot, Brussels, Belgium. (Author's photo)

As Lefebvre (1974/1991) states, "sovereignty implies 'space'" (280). As such, the struggle for autonomy entails a deep engagement with the spatiality and territoriality of that struggle. It also requires an examination of what political sovereignty is and does and how it might (or might not) facilitate food sovereignty. *We Want Land to Live* reads the discourse and practice of food sovereignty through, with, and against social and political theory to describe and explain spatial and territorial strategies to foster life in the margins of the corporate food regime. The margins are exemplified in the community permaculture garden in figure 1, which is in a vacant lot behind a wall; it is a narrow slice of green in between two buildings, and it is never not threatened by development. In keeping with theories of power that frame resistance as networked and partial (Foucault, 2003), I aim to advance an understanding of food sovereignty in the "Global North" as a biopolitical struggle in which activists claim space for life in deeply relational, highly contingent, and often temporary ways.

Food sovereignty, as described in this book, mobilizes a particular kind of oppositional power through marginality (Scott, 2008). Spatial strategies are key to mobilizing contentious politics (Martin & Miller, 2003), because all spaces, especially those mobilized in struggle, are neither fixed nor absolute (Massey, 2005). Space is held together through the process of being made and unmade; it is temporary, transformative, and subversive in multiple dimensions. Massey (2005) writes that "any politics which acknowledges the openness of the future . . . entails a radically open time-space, a space which is always being made" (189). These basic principles foreground politics that recognize how power is shared, not possessed, and understand that change takes place by collaboratively transforming already existing spaces into what McKittrick (2006) calls "more humanly workable geographies" (xii). I have come to think of these politics in my own work as "radical collectivism"[2]—political economic space generated through mutuality and self-determination, operationalized through relations of love.

While my theoretical engagements are decidedly poststructuralist, the research is resonant with Marx's "agrarian question," with which he queries whether and how capitalism relates to the peasantry and also how it articulates with the more "recalcitrant" biological bases of agriculture, such as seeds and animals (Goodman & Watts, 1997). Kautsky (1988) elaborates on this by inquiring specifically into "whether, and how, capital is seizing hold of agriculture, revolutionizing it, making old forms of production and property untenable and creating the necessity for new ones" (12). I engage with agrarian studies literature in framing the problems that food sovereignty identifies, but most of the solutions that are sought by the practitioners of food sovereignty as I have observed them in the United States and Europe are partial, contested, capillary, and networked, as opposed to class based or movement based. Food sovereignty's relationship to the agrarian question deserves more attention than I can give it here, but I do hope my contribution to this debate is to show that food sovereignty often seeks answers to old questions in ways that are innovative and thought provoking.

The title of the book takes its inspiration from the last, summary paragraph of the response by nongovernmental organizations (NGOs) to the Rome Declaration on World Food Security at the World Food Summit in 1996, at which the concept *food sovereignty* was articulated in various documents by La Via Campesina.[3] The final statement of the response is a condemnation of states and supranational organizations for their failures to provide real and lasting food security for the world's poor. It outlines six key elements of a model for an alternative food system, the first three of which propose to redress inequalities in access to productive resources such as land. After elaborating on the idea that the root of hunger lies in injustice and that changing this lies in privileging life over profit, the statement concludes, "Our message is simple: *Queremos una tierra para vivir.*" Literally translated as "We want land to live," this statement captures two powerful geographic ideas, one material, one figurative, that drive food sovereignty practice: food sovereigntists demand not only the physical spaces to grow and consume food but also the political space for life.

Food Sovereignty, the Global South, and the Global North

Food sovereignty is discursively framed and mobilized through debates and exchanges between farmers and peasants in both the Global South and North (Desmarais, 2007). Such exchanges have been facilitated by the peasant organization La Via Campesina (LVC), a movement started in Belgium in the early 1990s by a group of farmers' representatives in response to the diminishment of platforms for dialogue about the needs of the world's small-scale farmers. LVC defines itself as the "international movement which defends . . . small-scale sustainable agriculture as a way to promote social justice and dignity. It strongly opposes corporate driven agriculture and transnational companies that are destroying people and nature" (LVC, 2012). The movement is composed of 150 local and national organizations in seventy countries from all the major world regions and represents about two hundred million farmers. LVC documents describe it as "an autonomous, pluralist and multicultural movement, independent from any political, economic or other type of affiliation" (LVC, 2012). LVC's local affiliates work on a variety of campaigns, including anti-GMO activism, gender equity, and agrarian reform (Desmarais, 2012).

According to some origin stories, food sovereignty first emerged as a concept and strategy in the NGO response to the Rome Declaration on World Food Security. This declaration was preceded by a discussion among farmers and peasants at LVC's second international conference in Mexico, during which the significance of food sovereignty for the NGO response was heavily debated (Desmarais, 2007). Ultimately positioned as a "civil society proposal to achieve food security," food sovereignty appears in article 6 of the NGO response as part of a package of rights to food that "take precedence over macro-economic policies and trade liberalization." In this document, food is defined as something that cannot be commodified because of its cultural context and social significance. Since this first declaration, through ongoing discussion, debate, and struggle, food sovereignty has seen considerable development (and modification) as a concept, as well as significant mobilization as a political strategy in both the Global South and North, particularly in Europe.

The launch of the U.S. Food Sovereignty Alliance in 2010 in New Orleans and the passage of the so-called food sovereignty ordinances in Maine in 2011 made it clear that food sovereignty had arrived as part of the food movement in the United States. In the past several years, food sovereignty–oriented activities, such as the expansion of urban agriculture, have proliferated in the United States and Europe. The ideologies that inspire these efforts in the Global North, as well as how they resonate with global activism in the South, cause no small amount of confusion and some tension in debates about what food sovereignty is or does. Literature addressing the ideas and practices of food sovereignty is emergent, but thus far a considerable amount of empirical and theoretical slippage exists in and between narratives about what constitutes food sovereignty, as well as how it translates across space and between territorial nation-states. This book aims to develop an understanding of food sovereignty that bridges North and South without detracting from the place-specific ways in which it proliferates. In theory, the struggle for political autonomy to realize the right to food and life is a universal one. However, the corporate food regime dominates differently in different places and is therefore constitutive of different strategies of resistance. In this book I hope to provide a nuanced perspective on food sovereignty as a global struggle for the space for life that takes a variety of forms in place-specific ways.

Food sovereignty works to break down North/South dualisms, which are a product of and constitutive of imperialism, the perpetuation of settler colonialism, and the existence of extractive corporate food regimes. For obvious reasons, I am reluctant to reify this rather specious dichotomy, and I actively work against its construction. That said, the discourse of food sovereignty emerged from peasant organizations acting in economically and politically marginalized places that are collectively referred to as the Global South, while many of the practices of food sovereignty informing the analytical framework I develop in this book are strategies employed in the context of postindustrial economies and societies in Europe and North America. My aim is not to co-opt this movement in a "Northern" context but to elaborate on how that narrative has taken root and resonated with people in places far from its origin.

The analytical framework I develop and deploy in this book stands on four themes (legs, if you will) identified in food sovereignty declarations and calls to action. They include work for (1) political autonomy, (2) postcapitalist economies, (3) sociocultural change, and (4) new food production models. The Nyéléni Declaration calls for "political sovereignty of peoples" (Nyéléni, 2007: 5) as a prerequisite for food sovereignty and identifies autonomy as a practice for realizing sovereignty.[4] Article 6 of the NGO response to the Rome Declaration on World Food Security asserts a demand for decommodified or noncommodified food production, arguing that "food cannot be considered as a commodity, because of its social and cultural dimension." All food sovereignty declarations seek social transformation, but nowhere is it more pointedly addressed than in the Nyéléni Declaration (2007), which states, "Food sovereignty implies new social relations free of oppression and inequality between men and women, peoples, racial groups, social and economic classes and generations" (9). Food sovereignty requires new modes of production that incorporate "ecologically sensitive production and harvesting" and that are sustained through "solidarity economies" and "under local control" (Nyéléni, 2007: 42). While the ambitious agenda of food sovereignty is likely to be difficult to realize in practice, it is powerful in the way in which it calls something into being and presents it as a legitimate vision of the world.

Marc Edelman (2014) urges "proponents [of food sovereignty] to sharpen their critical focus and acknowledge how daunting the challenges are" (960). This book contributes to this effort by offering a critical perspective, albeit one that is grounded in a position of advocacy and support. I aim to respond to some criticisms of food sovereignty but also to extend my own critiques of how food sovereignty's radical vision risks being co-opted by the powers it sets out to contest.[5] I aim to showcase groups that work within the constraints of the current political-economic-social system to offer alternatives that advance autonomy in keeping with democratic and ecological principles. I also suggest that food sovereignty cannot function within the modern liberal state but that its theory and practice outline the contours of an alternative political space in which life can flourish.

Research and Methods

The research informing this project began in 2009 and has not really stopped. My primary objective in the beginning was to understand everyday strategies of claiming power over and for life in the food system. The research questions animating my investigations thus include understanding the spaces that food sovereignty produces, how power is mobilized within them, and what food sovereignty looks like in them. Because the questions I ask are discursive in nature and invoke a geographical imaginary, the research relied primarily on a qualitative methodology. As such, ethnographic methods of participant observation, field notes, and interviews, both formal and informal, were my most frequently deployed tools of data collection. This book is based on over a hundred interviews and countless conversations with activists, gardeners, farmers, seed keepers, and community organizers working for and with organizations dedicated to food sovereignty.

Due to the global nature of food sovereignty discourse and practice, the research draws methodologically from ideas of global ethnography (Burawoy, 2000). This approach aims to reveal how actors at a local scale use economic and political processes to materially produce and discursively deploy narratives about globalization or global social movements (Gille & Riain, 2002). Unlike more traditional ethnography, global ethnography allows for the examination of the constructed nature of power relations in a wider spatial field than a village or a community. This is what Burawoy (2002) calls a "field," which can be thought of as the relations between sites rather than the sites themselves. In this case, the field is constructed of several dispersed field sites that tell a larger story than any one site could tell alone.

Because the range of potential field sites is vast, the qualifications for inclusion in the research project were threefold and related both to feasibility and representativeness. To be included in the study, each site had to demonstrate some evidence of food sovereignty activities, defined as collective action toward the decommodification of food and the democratization of the food system, per the food sovereignty narratives described previously. Each site also had to articulate in some way with the larger narrative of food sovereignty, either through written documents or verbal communication. Finally, the site needed to be accessible to me as well as to allow me to maintain long-term relationships with people living there.

Four field sites anchor the chapters in this book. The first is an urban garden in Lisbon, Portugal, which I came to know about in 2010 when I visited a colleague involved with it. My relationship with the gardeners continued in the aftermath of the garden's demolition. I also report on several urban garden projects I visited and a permaculture festival I attended while in Belgium in 2010. The second field site is a collection of communities in the Blue Hill area of northeastern Maine, where the so-called food sovereignty ordinances were first drafted and passed at the township level in 2011. My relationship with organizers in this community began in 2013, when I conducted fieldwork in the area. The third case is the White Earth Anishinabek reservation in northern Minnesota, which is home to the White Earth Land Recovery Project (WELRP), an organization overtly dedicated to food sovereignty. I grew up on a farm within a few miles of the reservation, although I knew little about it until later in life. I worked for two months as a volunteer for WELRP in 2010 and returned to do fieldwork in the summers of 2013 and 2014. The fourth case is my current home of Athens, Georgia, which has a burgeoning local food movement and is home to a variety of projects aimed at increasing food access for the urban population. The case considered here is a permaculture garden installed in a historically black neighborhood of Athens with a high rate of poverty, food insecurity, and homelessness. I have been involved with the project in various capacities since its inception in 2009.

The primary mode of data analysis and interpretation is a form of inductive content analysis of narrative data (LeCompte & Schensul, 1999). The data include transcribed field notes produced through more than a year of participant observation and hundreds of formal and informal interviews, some of which were audio recorded, translated as appropriate, and transcribed, as well as documents such as La Via Campesina's food sovereignty declarations. Qualitative data analysis involved an iterative generation of themes, which eventually framed the chapters in the book. For presentation purposes, the chapters are organized somewhat by theme, with each presenting an exemplary case study, but cross-fertilization is common and some cases appear in multiple chapters.

The book employs a dialectical approach to theoretical engagement and development; a robust body of food sovereignty literature does not yet exist, and what does is largely untheorized. Thus this research was as much about a search for theory as it was a search for practice. Grounded theory (Strauss

& Corbin, 1990) is practice in search of a theory, while inductive analysis is theory in search of practice. I tack back and forth between these two modes of reasoning throughout this narrative, because I feel that neither position tells much of the story. Most of the food sovereignty literature either generalizes the movement, glossing over its internal contradictions, or trends toward militant particularism, ignoring the broader implications of individual political stances on land, life, and seed. Theories of sovereignty in political geography have much to say about power in space and go beyond mere explanation to facilitate analysis. Specific instances of food sovereignty likewise have much to say about how to practice and understand autonomous food production but are not linked to larger systems that shape its existence and possibility.

Positional Awareness

As a feminist geographer, I am concerned with issues of power in research as well as how my position influences how I know what I know. My family arrived in northern Minnesota as back-to-the-landers and settler colonists of a small farm during the 1980s. My mother was a single woman farmer and ran our subsistence farm with help from me, my brother, and our neighbors. We had goats and chickens for our main sources of protein, in the form of milk, meat, and eggs. We briefly raised rabbits for meat and sheep for wool, but my attachment to the former and the relative stupidity of the latter made them a one-season experiment.[6] We shared a buck goat with several of our neighbors for breeding purposes. We heated our house with wood and cut firewood out of our one hundred acres of forest. My brother hunted deer in those woods and fished in the lakes. We also had a very large garden that met most of our food needs. We bred our own animals, butchering and eating the male offspring and retaining the female chickens for eggs and the female goats for milk.

We relied heavily on the help of our neighbors (the nearest more than two miles away), sharing labor when we butchered goats or harvested firewood and resources such as log-splitting or hay baling equipment. This cooperative community lifestyle came to an end when my mother married a corn and soybean farmer from the southern part of the state. We moved the summer I turned thirteen, and her role as a farmer came to an abrupt halt. She maintained a garden, but there were no more animals. We lived closer to town (six miles versus twenty), and so the grocery store became a more significant source for our food. This transition from subsistence to commercial agriculture and the change in gender roles that I observed made for an enduring topic of graduate study for me (see Trauger, 2007).

To say that I am familiar with the practice and philosophy of food sovereignty would be an understatement. I was raised in what most would say characterizes the best practices of postcapitalist food production and distribution: a female head of household, a shared economy of labor and resources, an unregulated gift economy with uninspected meat, raw milk, and fresh eggs from a free-ranging, self-sustaining flock of hens. Had we sold one unit of food, we would have been obliged to submit to some kind of regulation and inspection, but to my knowledge, no money ever changed hands for any unit of food or labor. I was raised in an economy based on mutuality, trust, and interdependence rather than competition, profit, and independence. It worked, even though there were moments of tension and struggle, particularly regarding my mother's unmarried status.

I include this lengthy and detailed genealogy of my farming life because it is notable and relevant for this book in a few different ways. First, my experience taught me that the way in which capitalism works to create consumers out of producers is insidious and ubiquitous. Resistance is almost always futile. My own mother, who fed a family of three from only her own labor and land, now grows a nearly symbolic (albeit productive) garden and purchases most of the food she and her husband eat. Her conversion from a peasant to a consumer is nearly complete. Second, everyone in my family looks at me like I have six heads when I say I want to be a farmer, and they always have, employing very specific gendered and classed rationales. Based on these rationales, all of my family's farms (four to date), and consequently the means of production for subsistence, have been lost to me, even though, as a settler, they never really belonged to me at all. Last, in spite of the profound losses of land I've experienced, I feel lucky to have learned what I did as one of the last peasants, albeit a settler colonist, in my family. Because of my persistence and my unwillingness to let gardening and homesteading go out of my life, I am a carrier of knowledge rapidly being lost.

I continue in this tradition at the time of this writing on my urban homestead that at one time was complete with illegal backyard chickens, illegal bees, and an illegal permaculture garden. Until 2015, Athens's arcane zoning laws banned any plant of any kind on lots under one acre, but there was no political will to enforce them. As long as I did not sell any produce, I was not in violation of any other law. My chickens were similarly banned on lots of the same size, but again, enforcement of the zoning ordinances was "complaint driven." Because I carry on the fine tradition of the gift economy with my neighbors, I kept chickens without incident until 2014.[7] In another form of civil disobedience, I purchase raw milk, which is illegal to consume in Georgia. I say consume because it is legal to purchase it as "pet food," just not to consume it as a human. I procure this banned substance from a local farmer, who always has a smile and a kind word for my four-year-old "pet," who drinks about a half gallon each week. I do this not just as a matter of politics.

I have juvenile diabetes, which is an autoimmune disease with a heritable predisposition, very likely brought about by exposure to endocrine-disrupting chemicals such as pesticides and plasticizers (Guthman, 2011).[8] There is research indicating that half of all Holstein cows—which historically have produced the majority of conventional and organic milk in the United States—have a protein in their milk that may trigger an autoimmune response in individuals predisposed to juvenile diabetes (Laugesen & Elliott, 2003). The only milk I can put in my daughter's body with confidence that it has not come from a Holstein is milk directly purchased from a farmer. The source of my milk, a Jersey cow named Maybelle, is a visible presence at the farm where I go each Saturday to pick it up. I scratch Maybelle's back while she eats lush green grass with her calf still at her side. Her glossy brown-black coat gleams in the sunshine and I pity her industrialized cousins, knee deep in filth. I believe that I have a morally supported universal right to this health-sustaining milk for my daughter and that she has a right to be healthy. The FDA and the State of Georgia disagree. In a ruling in 2011, a federal court held that there is no general, recognizable right to consume foods of one's choosing or rights to physical health related to diet, specifically raw milk (Kurtz, Trauger & Passidomo, 2013).

Because of all this, I am neither a neutral nor an objective observer of food sovereignty, and I do not wish to be. This makes me the best and the worst person to study it, depending on where one stands on the accepted politics of science. Not only do I have deep working knowledge of the practices of food sovereignty, I also have a strong political commitment to encouraging them to continue. I have a profound emotional connection to food sovereignty as well— based not only in my past but in my present, in the lives of my chickens, the life of my garden, and my daughter's health. I do not, and I choose not, to view the animals, soil, and people who shape my life and the people and places that shape this research as part of a subject-object binary in which my corporeal health is distinguishable from any other's. We are all in this together.

On that note, I want to call attention to the extractive potentialities of social science research and acknowledge the unevenness of the benefits that accrue from my work with the people (and other living things) who appear in the pages of this book. While my career may benefit from the publication of this book, which is informed by the lives of those who contributed to it, at best, their lives will not necessarily be impacted in any significant way by it. I have written elsewhere about resolving this troubling conundrum (Trauger & Fluri, 2014). I hope and intend to position myself not as someone who speaks "for" any particular group but rather as one "speaking with" (Nagar, 2014) those who seek autonomy and rights within the food system. In that spirit, I stand with the White Earth Tribe (and many others) in Minnesota in opposition to the construction of a tar sands pipeline across the headwaters of the Mississippi River and over countless ricing ponds. I will contribute royalties from this book to that effort, as well as to ongoing efforts to reclaim and return land to the Anishinabek, who were forced off the land on which I was raised.

Embracing a plurality of ways of knowing through my involvement with farmers, eaters, and the life that sustains us has shaped my interaction with the contemporary food system in profound ways for most of my life. I believe that the state of my health is directly linked to policies that favor industrialization and thus exposure to endocrine-disrupting chemicals, and I have more faith in my farmer's concern for my health than my government's concern for it. I have learned nearly everything I know (and believe to be true) about food sovereignty by being a practitioner and by supporting (in various ways) those who seek it out. This relational and intersubjective way of knowing is a kind of knowledge not always welcomed in the scientific contexts in which I often write, perhaps even the institution that seeks to publish this book. It is, however, a critical viewpoint, an alternative episteme, and an ontological rupture that I find to be important and necessary.

Organization of the Book

In chapter 1 I provide a history of food sovereignty in both the Global South and the North, beginning with a discussion of the globalization of agriculture and the subsequent corporate monopolization of power over the food system that led to food sovereignty activism as a particular kind of response to the failures of previous food justice activism. This chapter engages with food regime theory, which posits that modernist development trajectories impoverish populations and restructure territory in the countryside as a strategy of accumulation by dispossession. I also engage theories of sovereignty to identify the state as a political actor coproduced by transnational capital with the power to create a "state of exception" (Agamben, 2005) over life and death. Chapter 1 relies on documents and declarations that emerged from various food summits as well as other literatures detailing the history of La Via Campesina and other international and domestic organizations that have emerged in response to the capitalization and globalization of agriculture.

In chapter 2 I discuss episteme, ontology, and epistemology to think through how food sovereignty defines and categorizes nature and culture: the political, social, and economic. I argue that food sovereigntists reinvent the ontology of food production and distribution through blurring the binaries—such as urban and rural, nature and culture, producer and consumer—that characterize the modernist food system. In this chapter I lay out a rationale for understanding food sovereignty as an alternative production model premised on permaculture practices (often in urban space) that is based on mutualist exchange, social transformation, and self-determination. From this basis, I argue that food sovereignty is part of a definitional struggle over the meanings of life and death in the food system, and I theoretically position food sovereignty as a radical and collective struggle for alternative political spaces outside the current governance but still within the territorial bounds of the modern liberal state.

In chapters 3 and 4 I elaborate on how space and territory are critical to the food sovereignty project and how all social struggles are necessarily spatial ones. Chapter 3 uses the case of an urban garden in Lisbon, Portugal, to investigate how food sovereignty subverts normative urban landscapes with permaculture gardens. Coincident with the modernist development project, public spaces (and the rights associated with them in democracies) are eroding into dead public spaces dedicated to the accumulation of capital (Sennett, 1974/1992). Food sovereigntists challenge normative assumptions about urban space by exchanging food and seed in alternative modes of distribution, often on collectively held lands. These spatial strategies—which are often temporary—are resonant with "freezones," spaces dedicated to creating spaces of freedom, self-reliance, and mutual aid (Bishop & Williams, 2012). The temporary nature of these spaces reflects the limits of the power of the liberal state to decide the "exception."

In chapter 4 I discuss how food sovereigntists articulate rights claims on the basis of a morally universal right to life, and how that poses problems for formulating such claims as civil rights or political demands directed at the state. Food sovereignty is entangled in complex articulations of rights, both individual and collective, which are not well delineated in the literature. The demand for rights will always be at risk of failure and vulnerable to states of exception without the creation of political spaces at multiple spatial scales, often below and beyond the reach of the state. I position these politics within the narrative of insurgent or "agrarian" citizenship (Wittman, 2009), which places its allegiance with nature, community, and "life itself" rather than the state. This chapter will examine the food sovereignty ordinances enacted in several Maine townships and how their partial success reflects their incomplete articulation of collective rights for protection against the corporate food regime.

In chapters 5 and 6 I discuss how food sovereignty activism aims to change the economic value of food and thus, I argue, articulates a postcapitalist politics (Gibson-Graham, 2006) of food production and distribution. Chapter 5 takes up the persistence of noncommodified food exchanges on the White Earth Indian Reservation in Minnesota, which are used to facilitate food security. The examination of these practices reveals the way in which state-driven priorities, such as the preservation of resources for commercial and sport fishing, ricing, and hunting, criminalize Native activities. It also reveals how such priorities attempt to enroll tribal members in circuits of capital as consumers. The tribe resists through refusals to commodify wild rice and other foods and in so doing demonstrates the failures of what colonialism was supposed to do (Simpson, 2014). I draw on notions of gift economies to suggest that food security is achievable through community-based initiatives rather than accumulation as usual.

In chapter 6 I elaborate on the role permaculture plays in subverting state efforts to commodify seeds and criminalize seed saving. I use the example of a permaculture garden to suggest an alternative production model suitable for food sovereignty but also to highlight the profound alienation from capitalism and the state that led activists to choose this particular production practice. The use of permaculture as a food-production practice does not pose a material threat to capitalist agriculture; it offers an ontological alternative to privatization, consumption politics, and the commodification of food, which have plagued alternative food movements. I draw on anarchist social theory to suggest that hierarchies of authority in all forms need to be replaced with direct action and horizontal politics in order to allow autonomy.

In the conclusion I argue that food sovereignty, as a biopolitical and geopolitical struggle, constitutes a discursive *and* a material challenge to the corporate food regime. In this chapter I bring together various threads of social and political theory to speculate about the future of agriculture under food sovereignty as well as comment on how spatial strategies of food sovereignty may be used to understand and encourage other strategies for autonomy. Resistance to the (neo)liberal state in many ways coproduces its existence, and the production of alternative imaginaries of belonging outside of state/capital is already creating radical alternative futures within the "shell of the old" (Ince, 2012). These possibilities appear not without consequence on the political map, and as such, food sovereignty, with its attention to direct action and democracy, deserves attention as a potentially powerful force to transform the modern liberal state.

PART I

CHAPTER ONE

Political Economies of Food Sovereignty

What we said in 1997 is not [what] we say [food sovereignty] is now.
Paul Nicholson, La Via Campesina, 2013

The United Nations Declaration on Human Rights, article 25(1), asserts that "everyone has the right to a standard of living adequate for the health and well-being of himself and of his family, including food, clothing, housing." Yet, according to the UN Food and Agriculture Organization (UNFAO, 2013), an estimated 870 million people do not have enough food to meet their needs and suffer from chronic undernourishment. The vast majority of people suffering from hunger and hunger-related conditions live in the least developed countries, and all people who suffer from hunger in either the developed or the developing world live in extreme poverty. Many of those in the developing world are landless former peasants or farmers struggling to live off the exports of commodities to the Global North. Clearly, the right to food is not a guarantee, even for those who grow food; the right is available only to those who are willing and able to pay for (or otherwise receive as aid) legally sanctioned food.

The failures of food security and other policies to guarantee the right to food are at the heart of the radical reforms that food sovereignty demands in order to end hunger and secure sustainable livelihoods for small-scale farmers (Holt-Giménez & Shattuck, 2011). Food sovereignty narratives identify modern notions of property rights and global capitalist markets as the source of the problems in the food system. These narratives are clear that reform in the food system requires the rejection of the global market for commodities as a mechanism for food security, and they implicate the state for its policies that marginalize small producers (Nyéléni, 2007). The calls for radical solutions, however, do not adequately engage with the problems that the modernist liberal state presents for food sovereignty. Working through these gaps and omissions requires an understanding of what is meant by liberal sovereignty and how it works in relationship to power, territory, and rights.

But first, a history.

The Political Economic Context of
Food Sovereignty's Emergence

Many food sovereignty scholars identify the enclosure acts in Great Britain in the 1700s and 1800s, which privatized common lands and forced thousands of peasants off the land, as a pivotal moment in the modernization of agriculture (Dawson, 2010). Enclosure consolidated farmland in the hands of a few and induced thousands of workers, now without the means to produce for themselves, to work for wages in factories (Kropotkin, 1907). This spatial shift in landownership facilitated and paralleled the transition from agrarian, feudal (or otherwise "traditional") societies toward an urbanized, rationalized capitalist society structured politically through the nation-state and its biopolitical functions (Foucault, 1978; Habermas, 1987). According to Harvey (1990), "Scientific domination of nature promised freedom from scarcity, want and the arbitrariness of natural calamity" (12). Modernist assumptions about the separation of nature and society also normalized new allegiances to the state and its guarantee of food security through innovations in agricultural science (Russell, 1966).

The creation of subjects who value their identity as autonomous individuals politically allegiant to the nation-state and find fulfillment through capitalism is perhaps modernity's greatest accomplishment (Habermas, 1987; Appadurai, 1996). Modernity is also characterized by the production of unequal social relations, in particular the production of racial categories through natural science (Gilroy, 1993), as well as the gendered division of labor in the production of public and private space (Landes, 1988). Modernity, with its emphasis on urban dwelling and wage-labor relations, also constructs the urban-rural divide that normalizes the countryside as the ideal site for the peasantry and food production (Murdoch & Pratt, 1993). The power of this narrative has transformed societies everywhere, making peasants into laborers and farmers into entrepreneurs (Gidwani, 2008).

In the past sixty years agricultural production in nearly every part of the world transitioned to some degree to a modern agricultural system characterized by a vertically integrated market (versus a subsistence) economy of food (Friedmann, 1993). The commodification of food in this "second food regime" (Friedmann & McMichael, 1989) resulted in the vertical integration as well as a concentration of power among a few very large firms, with national governments increasingly tailoring food regulation to the demands of agribusiness. Decision-making power about some of the most fundamental aspects of life—land, seed, and food supplies—is now concentrated in the hands of national states, supranational organizations, and transnational corporations (Goodman & Watts, 1997). These institutions work together, largely through territorial state policies such as structural adjustment programs, to continue the process of enclosure and to enroll small-scale producers in the global economy (Patel & McMichael, 2009). This form of development had impoverished and made hungry millions of people by removing them from the land and into wage-labor relations in the global economy.

State-run food security programs, premised on the notion that people should have access to safe, adequate, and appropriate food, emerged with the development of the welfare state in the 1960s, primarily in more developed countries. In the United States, food security policies emerged as a response to both the over-production of commodities and widespread poverty during the Great Depression (Allen, 1999). This model has since expanded to many more nation-states, particularly during the Cold War era. Additionally, the technological changes brought to bear on agriculture via the Green Revolution in developing countries were an exercise in philanthrocapitalism justified by mitigating food insecurity (Morvaridi, 2012). The development of policies that employ market mechanisms to distribute food to the poor are consistent with microeconomic policies and neoliberal notions of the subject that make the individual responsible for nutritional intake via the purchase of food or the receipt of it as food aid (Barrett, 2002). Subsidies for commodities produced in the developed world also produce surplus to be used as a tool of foreign policy and artificially suppress food prices to facilitate growth and profit in other economic sectors (Selowsky, 1981).

Research shows that, in nearly every context, food aid alleviates the short-term need for food in an emergency but initiates a long-term pattern of dependence (Levinsohn & McMillan, 2007). The global circulation of commodities such as rice or maize reduces local prices, lowers farmers' incomes, and ultimately undermines domestic production. Both the depression in income and the loss of domestic production set up conditions for dependency on foreign sources of food. Additionally, policies such as subsidies for commodity production encourage oversupply in countries from which the aid comes, which creates systemic dependence and poverty. Export models of agricultural development, such as the production of coffee, also produce situations of vulnerability in which farmers can potentially grow a commodity they can neither consume nor sell if global prices decline below the costs of production. This means that both food aid (the production of consumers) and export-oriented models of development (the production of commodities) are part of the "spatial fix"—the transnational restructuring of space via capitalist transformation of rural agricultural spaces (Harvey, 2003).

Food safety legislation connects the capitalist transformation of agriculture to the state and its food security programs in tangible ways. Food safety standards are a key mechanism for governing global trade in commodities (Dunn, 2003). Harmonization between countries is specifically designed to reduce barriers to trade and promote free trade. Standards, however, when based on the science of hygiene or food safety, often facilitate the production of food in ways that benefit multinational capital and marginalize small-scale producers (Kurtz, Trauger, & Passidomo, 2013). Food safety legislation is an effective way for states to steer agricultural production toward large-scale production models, such as those privileged in the contentious Food Safety Modernization Act (FSMA) in the United States. The FSMA is designed to prevent food contamination rather than react to its occurrence. This means that food safety practices that were never appropriate for small-scale production and that are cost prohibitive for most farmers are now required, sparking widespread resistance from small-scale farmers.

Food security, through its market mechanisms, the (over)production of global commodities, and the territorial, state-based policies that promote it, requires dependency on the modernist industrial model of agriculture. These and other policies undermine the livelihoods of smallholders globally and generate new distances and inequities between producers and consumers. The state, through its policy mechanisms for food security or food safety, is a regulatory Trojan horse for promoting and continuing certain agricultural practices. The state also facilitates the accumulation of capital in the corporate sector, through the way in which new requirements act on and respond to strategic advantages already existing in commoditized, industrialized agriculture. While social movements have emerged to contest the corporate food regime, the state and the free markets it facilitates and enforces have blunted their political edge.

The Alternativeness of the Alternatives

Market relations are implicit in all the so-called sustainable alternatives that have emerged in the second half of the twentieth century (Buck, Getz, & Guthman, 1997; Hinrichs, 2000). The emergence of organic agriculture in the 1980s and its widespread adoption as a federal program in the 2000s signaled a change on the part of both producers and consumers to reject environmentally damaging practices, although sales of certified organic products remain small. The development of standards for Fair Trade similarly signaled a rejection, largely by consumers, of unfair labor practices and unfair prices for global commodities, such as coffee and bananas. Sales of Fair Trade products are higher in Europe than in the United States, and such products command a growing market share (Renard, 2003). The globalization of organic production and the success of the Fair Trade model fit well within the neoliberal global food economy.

Under these alternative models, consumers pay more for a product in the belief that they are "doing good," but they have little or no control over how the benefits are distributed or accrued on the other end of the supply chain (Trauger & Murphy, 2013). Far from addressing the failures of the market to ensure justice for consumers and producers, organic and Fair Trade have scaled up the governance of food from the state regulatory apparatus to supranational nongovernmental organizations that govern within voluntary auditing systems. These consumer-driven and market-based initiatives and their codification into labels and certifications only made organic and Fair Trade agriculture "safe for capitalism" (Guthman, 1998: 150). Other efforts to "draw attention to the severe shortcomings of commodifying food" (McMichael, 2009: 163) include civic agriculture (Lyson & Guptill, 2004) and the (re)localization of food production and consumption through "embedded" markets (Hinrichs, 2000; Winter, 2003).

Embedded or local food systems, however, have a tendency to produce a two-class food system in which those who produce the food cannot afford to purchase it. The production of inequality that persists in capitalism appears even in markets characterized by embeddedness, leaving middle-class consumers with more power and privilege than farmers or lower-income consumers (Hinrichs, 2000). Local food systems also trend toward a "defensive" (Winter, 2003) or "unreflexive" (DuPuis & Goodman, 2005) stance against global capitalism without interrogating how capitalist orientations in local markets reproduce the inequality that embeddedness set out to disrupt. The emphasis on the transformative potential of individual purchasing decisions in local and organic markets also is consistent with the neoliberal agenda of self-care and the modernist paradigm of individual autonomy and rationality (Guthman, 2008b).

Social movements on behalf of the poor and hungry often tend to see global markets as driving the production of inequities in the food system and to tailor their responses accordingly (Hinrichs, 2000; Levkoe, 2006). Food justice or community food security activism seeks to decommodify food, but it often includes charity as a troubling approach to food injustice (Anderson & Cook, 1999; Guthman, 2008b). Charity models are consistent with neoliberal food policies because the distributed foods are often surplus commodities, and their redistribution does not challenge the current economic structures of the food system that produce hunger and surplus in the first place (Poppendieck, 1999). Similarly, food justice movements that focus on equity as a goal are unclear or agnostic about what action is to be taken to achieve that goal (Gottlieb & Joshi, 2010) and often discipline individuals to be better neoliberal subjects (Guthman, 2008a; Slocum, Shannon, Cadieux, & Beckman, 2011). Additionally, very few, if any, forms of food activism specifically target neoliberal policies, and they thus fail to engage with the state-based policies that develop and promote markets (Alkon & Mares, 2012).

Holt-Giménez and Shattuck (2011) assert that the new "food movements" of the late twentieth century constitute a Polanyian "double movement" between regulation and free-market dynamics. Polanyi (1944) argued that capitalism needs regulation of capital to temper its tendency toward crisis. Deregulation often begets efforts at regulatory reform, while regulation foments resistance to restriction; hence the "double" movement. This complex interplay between market freedom and policy formation ensures the existence of the liberal state. According to Polanyi (1944), neither markets nor states can exist or persist without each other. Agricultural policy in northern economies is a case in point of the iterative nature of markets and states. Food sovereignty, according to Holt-Giménez and Shattuck (2011), is a response to the deregulation of agriculture brought about through neoliberal policies in the Global North that extend globally through transnational capital. Food sovereignty, however, envisions not more regulation of agriculture (i.e., food safety laws) but different kinds of rights, many of which provide protection from corporations (i.e., rights to determine trade) for small-scale farmers, indigenous people, and peasants (Brenni, 2015).

Defining Food Sovereignty

Since the mid-1990s, the concept of food sovereignty has gained considerable traction in a political struggle for progressive reform in the food system (Edelman, 2014). It has been widely adopted in a variety of places and contexts, and while it has been effective in mobilizing change, it is broad in its scope and ambition (Clapp, 2012). The degree to which food sovereignty has become used as a rallying cry for food justice the world over is laudable, but the very broadness of its vision also threatens to reduce it to an empty, shifting signifier (Edelman, 2014), leaving many to wonder what is actually meant by food sovereignty and by whom and on whose behalf it is to be employed. In fact, Edelman argues that contemporary usage (post-1996) of the term to call for radical change in the food system belies a very contradictory past, as well as its murky, perhaps less radical, origins in national food policy discussions in Mexico in the 1980s. He argues that food sovereignty now has a particular origin story that is effective in mobilizing the movement around a particular kind of politics.

This more commonly known origin story asserts that food sovereignty as a concept was first discussed by La Via Campesina at its second international conference in Mexico in 1996. It was then publicly unveiled several months later in the NGO Response to the Rome Declaration on World Food Security and in LVC's declaration "The Right to Produce and Access to Land" (Wittman, Desmarais, & Wiebe, 2010). These documents articulated food sovereignty as the "rights of nations" to determine their food systems and policies and the rights of peasants to produce food. The NGO response included a six-point plan for ending hunger and articulated the conditions under which food security might be achievable by and for nations. It includes strengthening the participation of farmers and NGOs in policy formation, reducing the concentration of wealth and power in corporations, strengthening the capacities of nations to provide food security, decreasing the detrimental environmental impacts of agriculture, and democratizing trade.

Edelman (2014) and others (Schanbacher, 2010; Patel, 2009) assert that in this document and in general, *food sovereignty* is positioned against *food security*. In the NGO statement, however, food sovereignty is identified as a *prerequisite* to achieving food security. Article 6 states that "international law must guarantee the right to food, ensuring that food sovereignty takes precedence over macro-economic policies and trade liberalization." Point 6.1 declares that "each nation must have the right to achieve the level of food sufficiency and nutritional quality it considers appropriate without suffering retaliation of any kind." Point 6.2 asserts that "all countries and peoples have the right to develop their own agriculture. Agriculture fulfills multiple functions, all essential to achieving food security." Far from presenting their goals as the antithesis of food security, food sovereignty advocates demand the political rights to self-determination and autonomy that are prerequisites, in their view, for food security.

This first declaration of food sovereignty was subsequently elaborated on in various meetings of NGOs and civil society organizations at various meetings. These include the Foro Mundial in 2001, the meeting in Sélingué, Mali, in 2007 from which the Nyéléni Declaration emerged, and a meeting of La Via Campesina in 2012. The Nyéléni Declaration (2007) articulated the most frequently invoked definition of food sovereignty, which is:

> Food sovereignty is the right of peoples to healthy and culturally appropriate food produced through ecologically sound and sustainable methods, and their right to define their own food and agriculture systems. It puts the aspirations and needs of those who produce, distribute and consume food at the heart of food systems and policies rather than the demands of markets and corporations.

Agarwal (2014) notes that this shift in focus from "nations" in 1996 to "peoples" in 2007 is significant in that it positions food sovereignty as all-encompassing, embracing everyone in the food chain as a potentially powerful actor.[1] The shift from "nations" to "peoples" is not just a semantic move to make food sovereignty more inclusive, however. It also signals a shift from disentangling national-scale food policies from transnational capital (goals that take up three of the six points in the 1996 declaration) to an interest in local action to assert, generate, and sustain political autonomy at multiple scales.

The Nyéléni Declaration marks a key moment in transnational organizing. It brought together a select group of five hundred delegates from a variety of organizations in eighty different countries to specifically address how to craft an international agenda for resistance to and independence from the influence of transnational capital in agriculture. In the Nyéléni Declaration (2007) of food sovereignty, the interests and rights of producers, distributors, and consumers are privileged, as is the ability of "local communities" to determine their food systems (13). It also includes a "right to food security"; the transformation of social relationships, particularly between genders and races; and the "sharing of productive resources," free from threats of "expulsion and privatization" (13). This declaration suggests a questioning of the modernization of agriculture and a rethinking of what the Nyéléni Declaration calls the "whole fabric of global economics and society" (17).

THE NYÉLÉNI DEFINITIONS

Delegates to the Nyéléni forum in Mali identified seven general areas of modernist agriculture that are constitutive of the problem of food insecurity and identified how these areas might be changed to facilitate political autonomy in the name of food security.[2] Working groups convened to answer questions about what food sovereignty is "fighting for" and "fighting against" and "what we can do about it" (Nyéléni, 2007: 25). For the purposes of the arguments I advance in this book I will elaborate on four themes: (1) local markets and international trade, (2) access to and control over natural resources, (3) sharing territories and land, and (4) production models.

LOCAL MARKETS AND INTERNATIONAL TRADE

Food sovereignty seeks to redefine relationships regarding markets, trade, and the exchange of food (Nyéléni, 2007: 25–27). The Nyéléni delegates argue that "currently trade is based on unsustainable production systems and is controlled by TNCs [transnational corporations]" (25). In the delegates' view, free trade policies have destroyed livelihoods and local economies. Neoliberalism, rather than guaranteeing the right to food, is in fact the source of food insecurity. The Nyéléni delegates recommend returning democratic control of food distribution to producers and consumers and contended that "autonomous control over local markets" (26) is crucial for achieving food sovereignty. They identify local food production, food cooperatives, local processing, and solidarity economies as key mechanisms toward this end. They also encourage "policies that protect local production and markets" and that work to "eliminate corporate control and facilitate community control" (27). Surplus, according to the delegates, is to be appropriated for the benefit of the community, if it is produced at all. In short, rescaling, decentralizing, and democratizing decision making about markets are required for autonomy.

ACCESS TO AND CONTROL OVER NATURAL RESOURCES

The Nyéléni declaration tackles the issue of land reform and the problem of privatization in radical ways (Nyéléni, 2007: 33–25). The delegates identify access to land as a key right required for food sovereignty, as well as recognizing that land is a resource that is unevenly distributed through discrimination against

the poor, women, and indigenous people. They write, "A genuine agrarian reform is needed that allows us continued rights of access to and control over our
territories" (33). They seek to "uphold the legal and customary rights of peoples
and communities for access to the local, communal resources" and include "access to and control over our seed varieties" (34) as a key element of autonomy.
They also identify an "alternative economic system among local producers" such
as that identified above as key to keeping land under community control. They
also seek to ensure women's access to land and work toward the recognition of
indigenous peoples as key actors in deciding issues of access and control over
all productive resources, including water, land, and seed. They conclude with a
simple statement: "We will fight privatization and patenting" (35).

SHARING TERRITORIES AND LAND

The Nyéléni Declaration also criticizes modernist political economic orientations toward territory that produce unequal social relations (Nyéléni, 2007:
35–27, 56–60). The Nyéléni delegates are clear about the way their episteme of
territory and power departs from the geographical imaginary of the nation-
state. They write, "We define territories beyond geopolitical boundaries" (35),
and they acknowledge traditional forms of knowledge, land use, and land access
rather than the rules of the nation-state. They stress "sharing territory" over
owning or privatizing territory and they resist "all forms of expulsion," whether
of indigenous people or migrants. Instead, they pledge to work to end discrimination, particularly against women, indigenous people, migrants, and future
generations, that keeps some people from accessing land. The Nyéléni delegates
also stress that traditional ecological knowledge, a strong civil society, and alternative economic systems are the basis for decision making over resources,
exchange, and conflict. They argue that conflicts over territories are generated
through privatization and liberalization of land markets that leave some with
much and many with too little. The key to making all of this possible is, they
conclude, "decision-making power at the local level" (60).

PRODUCTION MODELS

Food sovereignty is simply a discourse if it is not accompanied by agroecological practices that restore and regenerate soil and water and protect air quality.
Theme 7 of the Nyéléni Declaration identifies alternative production models
as key to accomplishing the objectives of food sovereignty. The delegates write
that food sovereignty is "rooted in environmentally sustainable production and
harvesting, under local control and honoring traditional knowledge" (42). They
identify the corporate and industrial model of agriculture as ecologically destructive and seek to replace it with one based on "cooperation and solidarity
between individuals and peoples" and one that "places biological and cultural
diversity above competition and specialization" (43). They stress democracy and

small-scale systems, while acknowledging that ideals for the sizes for farms and for democratic participation will vary from place to place. Rather than stipulate what form production should take, they identify the privatization of the commons, patriarchal control of production, and "laws and regulations which discriminate against artisanal and on-farm processing and local markets" (45) as the largest obstacles to realizing a more ecologically sensitive agriculture. They articulate a vision of "solidarity economies" in which food is prioritized within a community because it was produced in a way that protects the "fertility of the land" and "the integrity of seeds" (46).

As compelling as these visions are, they do not adequately confront the political realities of liberal sovereignty, namely, the territorialization of space and rights under the governance of the modern nation-state. Given that capitalism and liberal states have been mutually constituted in the project of modernity (Polanyi, 1944; Patel & McMichael, 2009; Barkan, 2013), any appeal to the state for rights that trump rights to private property or patents is paradoxical. Additionally, the appeal for expanded rights for farmers to control productive resources is clear, but very little is said about who or what could guarantee such rights (Patel, 2009; Schanbacher, 2010). Who will guarantee collective or usufruct rights that work against the interests of private capital, interests that the liberal state appears invested in upholding?[3] If such a rights guarantor exists, at what scale does it operate?

Although scholars agree that the radical demands of food sovereignty are disciplined and muted by the ongoing existence of the liberal structure of the state (Patel, 2009: 669), there is a tendency in much of the food sovereignty literature to continue to see the state as the guarantor of rights through more or different kinds of regulation. These arguments call for the use of territorial-state-based policies to displace the power of transnational capital, without addressing the fact that such policies may still drive and promote the circulation of transnational capital. There is, therefore, a fundamental tension between those who implicate the state-capital nexus of the corporate food regime as the problem and those who argue that the state can be a source of solutions. Resolving this tension is thought to be accomplished by enumerating additional rights for farmers. This solution does not question whether and how liberal democracy in the sovereign state as currently practiced may actually be part of the problem as well.

THEORIES OF SOVEREIGNTY

Sovereignty as a concept has long figured into geopolitical thought, particularly as it relates to the development of the modern nation-state after the Peace of Westphalia. Taylor (2000) defines sovereignty "as a condition of final and absolute authority in a political community" (766). Typically (and historically) this political community has been the "nation," and sovereignty refers to the state's (sometimes democratic) control over a delimited territory. Historically, sovereignty territorialized the nation-state, both in terms of controlling what lies within its boundaries in its internal spatiality and in terms of its recipro-cal relations with other nation-states that recognize it (and are recognized) as sovereign in external relations (Brenner, 1999; Benhabib, 2004; Agnew, 2009). The powers that inhere to the sovereign state give it the right "to kill or to allow to live" (Mbembe, 2003: 11) that which it is able to "capture" or appropriate (Deleuze & Guattari, 1987), as well as the right to noninterference in these de-cisions by external actors (Storey, 2001). The sovereign right to kill cultivates a parallel function in the sovereign right to foster and manage life, or what Foucault (1978) refers to as biopower. The management of life as a power held by the state is predicated on the sovereign right to decide what constitutes life, which makes those it can "capture" subject to state valuations of life (Agamben, 2005). In short, the sovereign is that which holds the power to value and foster life according to the political or economic usefulness of its life (N. Rose, 2007).

The actual practice of sovereignty is far more contested than the discourses that surround it might suggest; sovereignty itself is rarely absolute (Agnew, 2009; Elden, 2010). While having real effects, sovereignty is a social construc-tion that makes the territorial national state possible (Storey, 2001; Nyers, 2006; Agnew, 2009). Nyers (2006) suggests that this fiction is a product of "statism" as a social movement, which is "so powerfully successful that the state has be-come normalized as the only authentic community that can serve as a site for political activity" (xii). The state is created through the repeated performance of activities that produce its powers, such as those associated with citizenship, allegiance, and belonging. Benhabib (2004) writes, "Citizenship and practices of political membership are the rituals through which the nation is reproduced spatially . . . to ensure the purity of the nation in time through the policing of its contacts and interactions in space" (18). Through this normalization and natu-ralization of the state, alternative political practices such as self-governance or popular self-rule are rendered "unacceptable or unthinkable" (Nyers, 2006, xii). What constitutes the normative (the order of the state) necessarily produces the nonnormative (the chaos outside the order of the state), which, according to Schmitt (1922), must be guarded against. The "state of exception," or totali-tarian rule, is thus invoked in emergency situations to prevent the collapse of the state into chaos (Schmitt, 1922). Agamben (2005) extends the idea of the state of exception to suggest that it is no longer necessary to invoke exceptions in emergencies; the current state of political affairs is one of the suspension of civil liberties in order to sustain the sovereign power of the state.

The degree to which territorial boundedness figures into the sovereign power of the state is a matter of much debate (Agnew, 2009; Ong, 2007). These debates reveal the way in which the myth of the territorial basis of the Westphalian state system is increasingly challenged and is being replaced with a network ontology in which sovereignty is an emergent property of social relations. In this model, sovereignty emerges from neoliberal economic relationships between states, which extend the reach, or hegemony, of individual national states into the economic or political space of other territorial states in imperial ways (Hardt & Negri, 2009; Agnew, 2009). Some would say that the rise of supranational arrangements constructs new geographies of power that erode the power of the territorial sovereign state (Anderson, 1996). Others, however, argue that the nation-state is often strengthened rather than weakened with the rise of globalization and that global capital mobilizes certain powers of the nation-state to control resources, territory, and people (Agnew, 2005; Watts, 2000; Ong, 2007). Without doubt, however, the contemporary era presents challenges to existing ideas about the spaces and territories of the nation-state, particularly with regard to what constitutes authority and autonomy over space in transnational, if not postnational, political arrangements (Appadurai, 2003; Benhabib, 2004). What remains is a carefully maintained fiction about the territorial basis of the sovereign state.

The state of exception, according to Ong (2007), is selectively used to generate "overlapping or variegated sovereignties" (19) in which there are exemptions to state sovereignty (for transnational corporations) to produce value for capital. Similarly, McCarthy & Prudham (2004) suggest that the meaning of neoliberalism emerges through its practice as a form of governance that facilitates the development of markets, rather than as a priori modes of governance that favor deregulation. Ong's (2007) framing of neoliberalism as a Schmittian state of exception allows for the creation of "sites of transformation where market-driven calculations are being introduced in the management of populations and the administration of special spaces" for capital (4). While Ong (2007) makes visible the links between transnational capital and state powers of exception, Barkan (2013) argues that the state and the corporate body have never been separate. In fact, "corporate capitalism emerges as a mode of liberal government" and this "clarifies how reforms unwittingly reinvest the sovereign power they seek to subvert" (9). Ong and Barkan advance an understanding of sovereignty that is bracketed from its basis as a singularity of power over territory, an understanding that also demonstrates how liberalism and transnational corporate capital are so deeply intertwined they cannot be approached as separate entities.

The framing of sovereignty as both partial in its exercise of control over territory and also produced in various ways through the action of transnational capital is instructive for understanding how the corporate food regime works through the state. It also helps us to understand why and how appeals to the liberal state for rights are not necessarily viable solutions to the ecological, social, and economic crises identified by food sovereigntists. Rights in a (neo)liberal state are required to be translated through a market-based economy so that they can continue to support the normal order of the state (i.e., private property, patents, development, taxation). Additionally, any alternatives that are not easily governed by the liberal state (i.e., open source seeds, gift economies, community gardens) are simply rendered illicit and illegitimate, thus criminalizing and "capturing" those who produce and exchange food in this way (van der Ploeg, 2009: 266).

The question food sovereignty asks is, how then to avoid capture? Liberal state sovereignty is a specifically spatial and social strategy mobilized by the modern state to claim territory and subject life within the bounds of that territory (and in some cases, beyond) to the biopolitical power of the state. Sovereignty, while having real effects, especially over the rights to foster life, is a contested social construction that produces "imaginaries" of subjection, boundedness, and power. As demonstrated by indigenous resistance and political action for alternative sovereignties, liberal state sovereignty is a continued failure (Simpson, 2014). Therefore, the exercise of sovereignty by the state over citizens is hardly absolute, and this partiality opens up opportunities to (re)territorialize space in resistance to what Nyers (2006) calls the "social movement of statism." Food sovereignty is a powerful narrative of alternative modernity (or antimodernity) that challenges the political practices that have failed to produce "freedom from want" (Harvey, 1990). The discourse of food sovereignty demands fundamentally antimodern decision-making arrangements by communities and for communities over land, water, and seed supplies—without which life is not possible (Wittman, Desmarais, & Wiebe, 2010).

A nonviolent challenge to modernity requires engaging with and transforming hegemonic notions of power and territory. When the myth of "statism" and the exceptionalism of modernity go unchallenged, neoliberal subjects can be led to believe that geopolitical power is fixed and total in its manifestations and that the opportunity for subverting hegemony is possible only through liberal reform of rights and policies. This totalizing myth of power persists even while food sovereigntists and indigenous scholars assert that there are possibilities and sites for transformation through alternative notions of territory and rights to land. These notions look to a postnational future of agrarian citizenship (Wittman, 2009) that makes communities, not states, responsible for food security. The narratives of food sovereignty also open a political possibility for creating a different kind of state, one that attends to the needs of small-scale producers, the poor, and nature. This can be done by reframing notions of territory, power, and rights and acting upon those reframed notions.

In 2008 Ecuador became the first country to codify food sovereignty in its constitution. The legislation includes a ban on transgenic seeds, restrictions on natural resource extraction in protected areas, and disincentives to monoculture agriculture. It also establishes barriers to food imports and encourages organic production and reforestation initiatives. The law draws on legislation that recognizes the "rights of nature"—a new strategy used to defend human and natural communities from environmental harm. Since 2008, Venezuela,

Mali, Bolivia, Nepal, and Senegal have integrated food sovereignty into their national constitutions or laws. What this means for the future of these states, which are likely legislating themselves out of an interconnected and interdependent global capitalist economy and potentially undermining the structures of liberal sovereignty, remains to be seen. What is evident from reading political theory against the actions of food sovereignty, however, is that the rights of community, such as those identified in the Maine food sovereignty ordinances or collective land rights, cannot be defended adequately if a national-scale constitution moots those rights.

Food sovereignty's actions constitute a reterritorialization of power that the liberal state may or may not have the political will to resist, even though such actions often present direct threats to the "social movement of statism." That said, while the state may look the other way from the reterritorializing of power for a time, resistance in the form of gardens or other land claims are almost always threatened and temporary. Thus, perhaps the most essential part of the process to shift the scale of decision making away from the state and toward communities, tribes, and cities is to see the state as mutable, flexible, and open to the democratic possibilities offered by food sovereignty. This may be possible if food sovereignty and its package of rights become part of the DNA of the state, rather than a series of additional rights tacked onto a liberal sovereign state. The neoliberal state remains a failed institution in terms of securing adequate food for its citizenry through market-oriented policies, and it may not be fixed through the addition of rights unless they strip the rights of capital.[4]

Food sovereignty is clear about decommodifying food and transforming the political economic foundations of the global food system and corporate food regime. Food sovereignty is also clear about the production of alternative subjectivities. Raj Patel (2009), for example, writes that for food sovereignty to achieve its aims, "every culture must, without exception, undergo transformation" (671). Food sovereignty is as much about changing systems of production as it is about something more fundamental and perhaps more ontologically threatening to capitalist modernity: the transformation of meaning, primarily around land, labor, and exchange. All of these differences set food sovereignty outside the existing social movements for change in the food system, in terms of both what is resisted and how it is resisted. The narrative is less about poor people having a right to food and more about how commodification of food harms people and their territories. It is about how people have rights to produce food and not just rights to consume (some) food. It is also a narrative about people having rights to a particular kind of life and corporations and transnational capital not having rights to interfere in the pursuit of that life. It is a much more fundamental narrative than other social movements have put forth, and it implicates both the state and capital for being complicit in bringing death and destruction to the food system. It also looks elsewhere for solutions.

CHAPTER TWO

Episteme(s) of Food Sovereignty

Without agroecology, food sovereignty is a slogan.
Without food sovereignty, agroecology is a technology.
Blain Snipstal, 2013

Over the last two decades in several states in Brazil, the MST (Movimento dos Trabalhadores Sem Terra; Landless Workers Movement) occupied unproductive land and established sustainable agriculture operations on it (Wolford, 2010). MST members squat on land in the belief that property rights are mutable social constructions that stem from working the land, not owning it. They act in the knowledge that they are legally supported by the Brazilian Constitution, which requires that land serve a "social function" (article 5, section XXIII.) The MST aims to enact agrarian reform—the redistribution of land from colonial elites back to those made landless through dispossession—but also to provide basic health care and education, often unavailable to sugarcane workers or other landless peasants. For their efforts they have been arrested, jailed, and sometimes gunned down by military police. In legal battles, Brazilian courts tend to rule in favor of the land-owners and to frame MST activists as dangerous criminals in their rulings against them. In a rare bright spot in this struggle, in 2013, 280 MST families were granted title to approximately five thousand acres of farmland in Bahia, on which they had been living and working for nearly twenty years (Araujo, 2013).

Food sovereigntists propose radical change in the food system through alternative ways of knowing and doing, as suggested by the quote from Snipstal above and as demonstrated by the MST. Snipstal refuses to divide food sovereignty into discourse and practice, asserting that each is meaningless and ineffective without the other. Given that appeals to the state for rights are subjected to the logic of capital accumulation, food sovereignty must do more than engage with alternative practices or markets, as the reform-based and progressive social movements that came before it did. As demonstrated by the MST, it must mobilize a range of methodological alternatives that are consistent with its discourse, such as direct action (as opposed to charity, market creation, or policy changes), civil disobedience (instead of complying with discriminatory laws), and mutual aid (instead of relying on top-down aid).

For these reasons, I contend that food sovereignty is something new and different from the food justice efforts that came before it. I also suggest that it's no mere collection of food system cranks; it is a life-and-death struggle over the organization of food production and distribution in a postmodern and post-capitalist food system. It is not just a material struggle, however. Food sovereignty is also part of a definitional struggle over the meanings of life and death in the food system, which requires scholars to engage with food sovereignty's ways of knowing. In what follows, I argue that food sovereignty (re)defines and reorients the relationships between nature and culture, the political and the economic, and the social and the cultural. In so doing, food sovereigntists invent new epistemes of food production and distribution (based on old ones) by collapsing the binaries that characterize the modernist food system.

The Politics of Seeing from Below

Engaging with questions of existence means interrogating the conditions of possibility for knowing, or "episteme" (Foucault, 2002). If we believe Latour (2004), we cannot escape the relationships that shape our knowledge of the world, as all knowledge is relationally produced. This process of becoming "affected" by the world, such that we produce knowledge based on our interactions and our relationships, means that we exist in an intersubjective world of interconnected knowers. Scientific knowledge, even though its theories of objective knowing resist this, is also based on a relational experience. We produce our epistemes, our ways of knowing, in contexts shaped by particular power and knowledge systems, which means that all knowledge is governed by "rules of construction and evaluation" (Faubion, 1994).

Epistemologies that privilege interconnection between knowers, including the subaltern, resist the silences, exclusions, and essentialist understandings of individuals and cultures that have characterized knowledge production in the modernist era (Semple, 1922; Sauer, 1925). Latour tackles the many binaries in modernist thinking by reconnecting two of the most fundamental ideas of the modern world: nature and culture. Latour (1993) writes, "*The very notion of culture is an artifact created by bracketing Nature off.* Cultures—different or universal—do not exist, any more than Nature does. There are only natures-cultures" (104, original emphasis). Latour argues that modernist attempts to separate (or "purify") nature position it as something that is "out there" and unrelated to the becoming of other actor networks.

The same can be said of the subject/object binary, which Latour (2004) argues positions a subject as preformed, disconnected, and somewhere "in there." He argues that modernist assumptions about knowledge posit that "learning is not essential to its becoming; the world is out there and affecting others is not essential to its essence" (4). Latour suggests, in opposition to this, that subjects and objects do not exist prior to their relationship; their meaningful existence is coproduced through their relational becoming. In the same way, nature-culture takes on meaning through relationships. Nonhuman and human actors become affected through their interactions; they "learn to become sensitive" to each other and thus exist suspended in a relational process (Latour, 2004: 19). This process of relational affecting produces what Foucault calls an "episteme" or "the 'apparatus' which makes possible the separation . . . of what may from what may not be characterized as scientific" (Foucault, 1991: 197). Modernist science would like there to be one episteme, characterized by the subject/object binary, but Foucault argues that several epistemes may coexist and interact at the same time, being parts of various power-knowledge systems.

Feminist geographers have long argued that power-knowledge systems are always deeply relational and that subject/object binaries are scientific fictions meant to prop up particular regimes of "truth" (Gibson-Graham, 1994; G. Rose, 1997; Massey, 2001; Moss, 2002). Haraway (1988) refers to this epistemological process as the "god trick" (581), which perpetuates the fallacy that everything can be seen from nowhere. Haraway suggests that power and knowledge are products of choices about "how to see" and "where to see from" (587), and she urges scientists to "see from below" (584). Rather than extracting and generating knowledge in the unlocateable space of the academy as a resource for the scientist, feminist epistemologies support the cocreation of knowledge with research participants (Trauger & Fluri, 2014).

Intersubjectivity and seeing from "below" also characterize the formation of community around particular kinds of knowledge, or what Rose and Novask (2004), in a medical context, refer to as "biosociality." Biosocial groups form around a biologically based concept of "a shared identity" (N. Rose, 2007: 134) to contest the hegemony of medical expertise, advocate for rights and services, and form communities based on intersubjective ways of knowing about health and disease, often through their own bodily experience of it. Biosociality is a key aspect of developing social spaces in which scientific ways of knowing are represented as potentially problematic, rather than universally accepted, truths. N. Rose (2007) calls this "citizenship from below" because it bases its knowledge in lived experience and in the process troubles accepted ways of knowing about biological realities. The aim of such activity is often to introduce controversy and doubt about the intentions and functions of state-sponsored science and policies that proceed from it.

The emergence of citizenship "from below" signals a diminishing faith in the state to sponsor or sanction practices that promote health or wellness in the population (Rabinow & Rose, 2006). The emergence of food sovereignty as an alternative episteme in the food system is often characterized by the formation of biosocial groups that reject biopolitical state power and encourage the flourishing of multiple modes of knowing, particularly around the relationship between society and the natural world. This has the effect of creating different lived material realities, but it also cultivates a different sort of allegiance—to nature, farmers, or community, and not the state.

How Do We Know Food Sovereignty?

Figueroa (2013) asserts that food is a "modality by which capitalism is lived, and made tangible in everyday practice" (1). The lived experience of food is, in her estimation, key to triumph in the struggle for food sovereignty. Thus how we know food sovereignty matters in terms of understanding it, but it also is central to engaging in the political context in which it unfolds. Food sovereignty might best be understood by its claim to political autonomy with certain distinguishing characteristics, namely its rejection of transnational capital and articulation of systemic change. However, identifying one definition of food sovereignty necessarily forecloses others, and as someone who knows food sovereignty through lived experience, I am understandably reluctant to do this. Also, politics operate on a wide spectrum, and there is no reason to believe that one political position defines food sovereignty in its entirety.

Thus, rather than identify one totalizing narrative about food sovereignty, as many others have argued against (Desmarais & Wittman, 2014), and in the spirit of the Nyéléni definitions, I identify food sovereignty as existing on a political spectrum, categorized by its different bandwidths with regard to what autonomy means in the food system. Any activism for food sovereignty takes a particular political position related to the roles of state and capital in the food system and thus acts from those viewpoints in specific sets of ways. From both my reading of the literature and my research, I identify three largely distinct orientations toward food sovereignty: national food self-sufficiency, rights-based resistance to the status quo, and autonomous food production. These stances roughly correspond to the reformist, progressive, and radical trends in the food system identified by Holt-Giménez and Shattuck (2011). See figure 2.

Holt-Giménez and Shattuck (2011) characterize the contemporary agrifood system as a product of two opposing forces: the corporate food regime and food movements. Within these two forces there are four general trends: (1) neoliberal and (2) reformist, which aim to prop up the corporate food regime, and (3) progressive and (4) radical, which both challenge the corporate food regime,

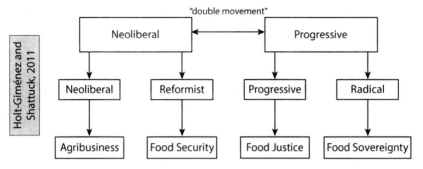

FIGURE 2. Food system regimes and trends. (Adapted from Holt-Giménez & Shattuck, 2011)

albeit in different ways. Within the progressive trend, food justice and food sovereignty seek to "introduce practical innovations for equity and sustainability to the food system, but also seek to change the structural conditions in which these innovations operate" (Holt-Giménez & Shattuck, 2011: 116). A key risk for progressives is the way in which markets co-opt and threaten the structural changes that are sought. According to Holt-Giménez and Shattuck (2011), "durable alliances" (109) between actors in the progressive and radical trends, such as the development of farm worker labor unions across agricultural sectors, are a central corrective to mission creep toward neoliberalism.

Radical trends in Holt-Giménez and Shattuck's model (2011) encompass objectives such as "dismantling corporate agri-foods monopolies, parity, redistributive land reform, protection from dumping and overproduction and community rights to water and seed" (129). Thus legislative reforms that are demanded in the more radical trend in the food system range from protecting smallholders' rights to self-governance to regulating international markets through supranational organizations and state-based policies. The radical trend, according to Holt-Giménez and Shattuck, includes both community-based rights through collective self-governance and the development of strong states and strong intrastate regulation—efforts that may in fact be in conflict with one another. In practice, the radical trend could include the illegal strategies employed by the MST of squatting on unproductive land and the reform of safety regulation to protect the interests of small-scale farmers.

This framing of food sovereignty encounters both the problems of the "big tent" (Patel, 2009), which makes food sovereignty all things to all people, as well as the problem of seeing the state as both the solution *and* the problem. It also suggests that there is a political spectrum along which a variety of forms of food sovereignty emerge, ranging from reform to radical. In what follows I elaborate on this spectrum, using Holt-Giménez and Shattuck's (2011) conceptual frame, beginning with what I identify as the most state-centric strategy, or a "reformist" tendency, which I call "national food self-sufficiency," designed to be achieved through policy. In the middle is "rights-based resistance," or strategies within the progressive trend that also appeal to rights from the state, but through forms of disobedience. In the "radical" trend I position "autonomous food production" strategies, which are used by people who are interested not in reform or resistance but rather in self-governance or, put more simply, political recognition of decision-making power over space and territory.

NATIONAL FOOD SELF-SUFFICIENCY

Food sovereignty is often situated as a response to "crises" in the food system, the global economic system, and the socioecological systems that support and sustain peasant agriculture (Rosset, 2008). In these narratives, dramatic collective action is called for, often in the form of public protests (sometimes dubbed "food" or "IMF" riots), to demand change (Holt-Giménez & Peabody, 2008). These changes include addressing the issue of power exercised by transnational capital, national state governments, and supranational organizations, which work together to marginalize agricultural producers (Bello, 2009; Patel & Mc-Michael, 2009). According to this literature, neocolonialism and globalization normalize modernist development paths that engage as many people as possible in urban and industrial sectors, accumulate through dispossession, and facilitate the capitalist transformation of the countryside (Bello, 2009; Pimbert, 2009).

Reclaiming control of production and distribution through regulation of trade by individual nation-states is seen as the solution to the crises precipitated by the transnational food regime. Thus in crisis narratives, food "sovereignty" is often used synonymously with food "self-sufficiency" on a national scale as a policy solution to hunger and poverty within the bounds of territorial national states (Shiva, 2004; Altieri & Nicholls, 2008; Bello, 2009). Crisis narratives largely mirror food sovereignty statements and declarations about the sources of and solutions to problems in the food system, but they do not pose any alternative other than a stronger, more self-sufficient, potentially protectionist state. Crisis narratives position the territorial state as an important actor in curbing the power of multinational corporations and supranational organizations, such as the IMF, and giving decision-making rights to peasants. This approach is vulnerable to co-optation and greenwashing by global capital because of the way the neoliberal state often governs trade and its people. In this sense, food sovereignty as national food self-sufficiency leans furthest toward neoliberalism on the spectrum, and it is vulnerable to failure for the same reasons that state-based food security policies have failed.

RIGHTS-BASED RESISTANCE

Declarations emerging from transnational food sovereignty organizations and other campaigns for autonomy in the food system often contain an appeal for rights to food. The UN Declaration on Human Rights is often invoked in rights narratives, as the declaration guarantees a right to food to all people, although this right often is not realized by many, especially the poor in the Global South. However, rights talk tends to get food sovereignty narratives into trouble for a variety of reasons already elaborated (i.e., who is the rights guarantor?) but also because when collective rights are stressed over individual ones, women, minorities, and the disempowered generally lose. Patel (2009) engages this troubling tension between individual and collective rights, writing, "I come down on one side of a broader series of debates on the tension between individual and collective human rights, arguing that in cases where group rights threaten individual ones, individual ones ought to trump" (671).

Thus rights narratives must critically examine the systems of power that rest on individual rights (Schanbacher, 2010; Wittman, Desmarais, & Wiebe, 2010). Rights narratives deployed in the Global North suggest that food sovereignty should work within the structure of liberal democracy to establish more rights for producers and other marginalized actors in the food system, such as rights to produce and consume food in ways that biosocial groups deem acceptable. These groups appeal to the state for rights and often attempt to influence legislation accordingly. While it is certainly safest (and easiest) to emphasize individual rights, where these efforts often lose political traction is through the emphasis on individual and atomized rights (i.e., farmers, consumers) versus a more collective approach to rights that include the rights of nature or entire communities. When it emphasizes individual rights, food sovereignty leans toward reform of the food system rather than transformation and could easily perpetuate potentially neoliberal politics of the individual (Alkon & Mares, 2012).

Human rights are a malleable social construction of the modern liberal state that place emphasis on economic privileges, such as rights to private property or access to natural resources (Charvet & Kaczynska-Nay, 2008). Rights are also conceptualized as creations of the social democratic state that were designed to counter the inequalities generated through the inauguration of global capitalist economies (Stammers, 1995). Claeys (2012) writes that La Via Campesina, as a movement advocating for food sovereignty, opposes both the authority of the state and market to control food production and the limited power that liberal or social democratic human rights guaranteed via the state can offer to peasants. LVC and other food sovereignty scholars suggest that food sovereigntists should look beyond the scale of the state to "communities, peoples, states and international bodies" (Nyéléni, 2007) and should "pluralize" the spaces of sovereignty (Hospes, 2014) in the search for rights. How then to find a new or different rights guarantor (Patel, 2009) to create new spaces for autonomy and to avoid the "institutionalization of human rights . . . that threatens their subversive potential" (Claeys, 2012: 852)?

AUTONOMOUS FOOD PRODUCTION

When policy reforms and "rights talk" fail, farmers, consumers, and activists take matters into their own hands. Pimbert (2008) calls this "autonomous food production" (3), in which self-governance is key to achieving the aims of food sovereignty. Pimbert draws on the writings of anarchist-Marxist philosopher Ivan Illich (1976), who identified autonomy as a condition of existence that allows a social group to identify their own needs and chart their own path toward meeting them. Pimbert asserts that industrial capitalism appropriates, via monopolies and commodities, the means by which people can "cope on their own, thus undermining freedom, independence and culture" (5). This approach to food sovereignty de-emphasizes the role of the state and rights and asserts self-governance and freedom as central to achieving a more just food system. In the context of the modern liberal state, this kind of action breaks across a right-left divide and includes both libertarian and anarchist approaches to food production and distribution.

Libertarian

Many advocates for food sovereignty are inspired by the libertarian Joel Salatin, a farmer and food sovereignty icon who writes prolifically about the way state and federal laws make local food production, processing, and distribution costly and virtually impossible for small-scale producers (Salatin, 2007). He appeared in the 2011 film *Farmageddon*, about food sovereignty, where he said,

> If I had one thing to say to the USDA and the FDA, I guess my question would be why do you hate freedom so much? What is it about freedom, whether it's the consumer's freedom to choose the food they want to drink, whether it's me as a farmer choosing the customer who wants to buy my product, or how I want to make my product? What is it about freedom that is so horrendous to you that you are willing to take my property, take my life, take my customers, take my animals, take my land, that you are willing to do this in order for me to not have the freedom to even sell a pork chop to my neighbor? (Canty, 2011)

This particular framing of "freedom" resonates with larger discontent with governance in the United States, exemplified by the Tea Party's libertarian politics. While marginal and radical, Salatin's views are often repeated among many in the alternative farming community. In this view, government does not need to be reformed, it needs to be minimized in terms of its involvement in food production. In this vision, however, individual rights (i.e., his right to sell a pork chop) take precedence over more collective rights to food and health.

Anarchist

Other approaches to food sovereignty take more anarchist angles. "Guerrilla gardens" temporarily, often overnight, turn urban space into gardens (Lamborn & Weinberg, 1999). Guerrilla gardening is widely practiced by food sovereigntists, as are other kinds of direct action, such as "seed bombing" or "PARKing Days." Guerrilla gardeners work under the assumption that their gardens or other installations may be forcibly removed by the city or state, and they function as both a definitional and material action to redefine the use of public space in cities (Chou, 2010). Rather than aiming for reform or realization of their rights, guerrilla gardeners take advantage of the fact that a city exercises incomplete or partial sovereignty over its territory. Anarchy in this sense rests on nonhierarchal, anticapitalist views and reframes land and space as communal, public, and open to political reinterpretation. Anarchist, autonomous food production undermines laws governing private property and challenges normative assumptions about where and how food can be produced and distributed.

Holt-Giménez and Shattuck (2011) warn against the co-opting tendencies of more reform-oriented and progressive trends aimed at changing the food system. They argue that collective strategies are key to advancing food regime change that will last. They and other agrofood-system theorists are concerned that the disappearance or weakening of the "left" in food politics endangers the radical change envisioned by food sovereigntists (McMichael & Myhre, 1991). Collective strategies work against the tendency toward neoliberalism in much of the food justice and alternative food networks activism and emphasize a different kind of politics that decenters the individual. The cases that compose the empirical section of this book thus focus on the struggle for *collective access to land* (in addition to individual ownership) and advocate for *collective rights* (in addition to individual rights), especially for rights to self-govern. In keeping with Holt-Giménez and Shattuck's language this strategy is something I've come to think of as "radical collectivism." (See figure 3.)

The cases in this book focus on creating and protecting either collective forms of production (chapters 3 and 6) or collective forms of distribution (chapters 4 and 5). The cases all feature people and communities who are fighting for the right to continue what they are doing, given that their strategies are currently criminalized. The activists in these cases also rarely hope for changes in policy at the scale of the nation-state, nor do they see it as necessarily a desirable kind of reform, and they do not see the state as willing or able to provide food security. The changes to the world that they envision articulate with larger-scale politics but are designed to take place at the scale of the garden, the tribe, or the township and often involve the use of public space as a broadly conceived "commons." Finally, they articulate a desire for systemic change—whether in the way land is accessed or in the way food security is achieved—and propose solutions so that "everyone does better when everyone does better."[1]

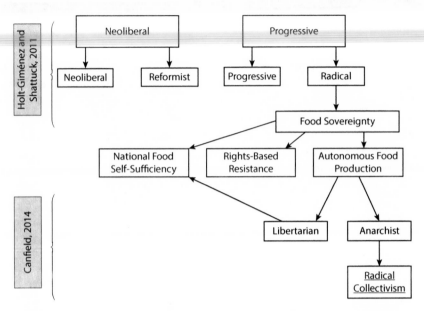

FIGURE 3. Typologies of political action for food sovereignty. (Adapted from Canfield, 2014)

Food Sovereignty as Radical Collectivism

A form of food sovereignty that creates "radical collectivism" refuses a Cartesian view of the world that is divided into the realms of the social, economic, political, and ecological. In this framing, food sovereignty is premised on the production practice of permaculture (often in urban, rather than rural, space), which recognizes the co-constitution of the natural and the cultural. It is also based on mutualist economic activities that work against the worldview that society is composed of atomized, rights-bearing individuals. Food sovereignty activism overtly aims to right the collective wrongs of the food system and advances a vision of social justice that requires complete transformation of society. A political space in which this vision for society can be realized allows collective rights to emerge through alternative ecological, economic, and social relations. In what follows, I elaborate on the vision that radical collectivism creates and works toward.

SOCIAL JUSTICE

Much of the literature on social justice discusses "distributive" justice, or that which is concerned with the equal distribution of "good and bads" in society (Miller, 1999: 1). This refers not only to social benefits such as access to education but also responsibilities, such as military service or care for the elderly. Another aspect of distributive justice is providing individuals with "rewards proportional to their contribution" (Tyler, 1999: 118). As such, distributive justice is concerned with achieving equity and preventing exploitation. Gottlieb and Joshi (2010) draw on distributive forms of justice for their work, identifying food justice as "ensuring that the benefits and risks of where, what, and how food is grown and produced, transported and distributed, and accessed and eaten, is shared fairly" (6). While their vision is consistent with various forms of alternative food systems, the strategies they identify do not challenge the political and economic structures from which food injustice and insecurity emerged.

Social justice is a key element of the Nyéléni documents and permeates that narrative throughout every theme and objective. It ranges from ensuring fair prices for producers to better working conditions for laborers, empowerment of women, care for migrants and indigenous people, and so on. Patel (2009) calls for no less than the complete transformation of society when he writes, with respect to women's rights, that "every culture must, without exception, undergo transformation" (671). While the hallmarks of distributive social justice—equal distribution of responsibility and benefits, broadening the scale and diversity of the community, and emphasizing cooperation (Barry, 1999)—are certainly desirable, food sovereignty's vision of social justice requires radical, systemic change. For example, better working conditions for farm laborers in the United States cannot proceed without fundamental change in political economic orientations toward migration and settler colonialism, dismantling monopoly control of agriculture, and shifts in property relations.

Justice, according to the people who appear in the cases in this book, is not about seeking a universal or normative form of justice (i.e., legal, institutional) but rather about the dismantling of the social, political, and institutional contexts in which social injustices are produced. This is not to say that other injustices are not produced in the process, but the food sovereignty activists featured in this book articulate an overt feeling of trying to right (collective) wrongs. In this book, these wrongs include demolition of gardens, unfair food safety laws, criminalization of harvesting and sharing wild foods, and the erosion of rights to seed saving. Social justice is seeking to rectify that wrong through (re)territorializing the commons, establishing rights to self-governance, and creating collective forms of production and distribution.

MUTUALISM

Food sovereignty narratives call for "alternative economic systems" and "solidarity economies" as necessary for changing an asymmetrical trade scheme. Food sovereignty also resists the production of inequality that so many local and organic food systems continue to perpetuate. J. K. Gibson-Graham (2006) suggests practicing this through the Nancian "being in common," achieved through the interdependence of a variety of economic subjects. This is accomplished via the conscious and deliberate (re)negotiation of foundational economic ideas and practices, the development of new economic languages, and the creation of new economic subjects. This strategy also engages with the principle of subsidiarity, which encourages decision making at the lowest scale and between the fewest people possible, such as agreements between producers and consumers about what food is safe to consume (Feagan, 2007). Given the legal option to do so, many communities can and do create systems that work against the inequality inherent in capitalism (Burke, 2012). Anticapitalist economies also often undermine state control of commerce by flying under the regulatory radar; in a (neo)liberal state, if something is not sold, it can't or won't be regulated.

Mutualism advances a classless society organized around collective possession of the means of production through use. Pierre Proudhon (1890/1966), for example, writes that property can be conditionally possessed so long as it is in use or occupied, much like the way the MST occupies unproductive land in Brazil. According to mutualist economic theory, the property legitimately belongs only to those who cultivate or otherwise use land. Land or other capital assumes value through use, rather than through ownership. Private property, according to mutualist economic theory, leads to a lack of freedom, the creation of a class system, hunger, and ultimately the destruction of society. Indeed, Proudhon calls private property "property as theft" that can be maintained only under state coercion.

Kevin Carson (2007) argues that "actually existing capitalism" is possible only through the interventions of the state in the form of subsidies and patents to corporations, military interventions as a key strategy to open international markets, and taxes and tariffs that privilege a powerful minority. Mutualism, as articulated by Carson, is a market in which labor is not separated from ownership and the generation of a class-based society and its associated inequalities would be impossible. He argues that a mutualist free market system would require notions of property rights, especially those related to land and intellectual property, that present alternatives to those on which capitalism is based. The ideas of property, trade, and credit articulated by the Nyéléni delegates suggest mutualist philosophies. Three cases in this book call for sharing land as commonly held and worked property in order to produce and share food rather than through private property and capitalist markets. The activists in the Maine case constitute an exception, in that they work to protect rights to buy and sell food, but they are collectively organized in order to grant themselves the power to govern the terms of production and distribution.

SELF-GOVERNANCE

Sovereignty is a form of self-governance, defined as autonomous self-rule at any political scale. It includes some kind of territorial claim as well as the "right to determine the terms of legal belonging" (Simpson, 2014: 10). Sovereignty is a tool variously used by nation-states to establish political authority, by indigenous groups to establish autonomy in the context of the end of colonial rule, by religious minorities demanding autonomy from the state, and by civil disobedients protesting the immorality of the state, such as the approach advocated by Thoreau. In a general sense, self-governing is the exercise of power without intervention from any other entity, including the state. Nation-state sovereignty is just one form of self-governing, but other kinds of "popular sovereignty" and democratic self-rule exist, sometimes as "overlapping sovereignties" within nation-states. Self-rule requires consensus decision making, codes of ethics, grievance procedures, a method for choosing rules, and a balance of power between competing interest groups within the community.

One of the more famous and somewhat successful instances of self-governance in a postcolonial context is the promotion of swaraj as a strategy in the Ghandian independence movement in India. *Swaraj* is a word of Hindi and Sanskrit origins meaning "self-rule" and, in the case of Ghandian independence movements, freedom from foreign domination. Key elements of swaraj are government structures that are not hierarchal but based in autonomous individual governance and capacity building through community-based organizations and nonprofits. Decentralization is a defining element of all forms of self-rule, and the swaraj movement in India emphasized independence not only from the British Empire but also from the social, cultural, economic, and political structures that compose Western state bureaucracies. The radical alternatives proposed by Ghandi have rarely been realized, but some of the social organizations shaping reforms of governance have been key to India's particular form of democracy.

To varying degrees, the cases outlined in this book articulate demands for self-governance. In some instances, the demands are to be left alone—to be allowed to continue to work the land in ways that support community and ecological health. In this sense, they seek freedom from state oversight and control, and their strategies and narratives about their politics are anarchic or libertarian in nature. They see the state as illegitimate and supporting capitalism over other economic forms. In other instances activists work to reshape the state, typically at lower scales of governance, such as the township or tribe. They work to reform governing processes from the inside out. In so doing, they articulate a different vision of democracy, one that responds to the needs of people rather than, in their view, corporations or narrowly defined private interests. All of the cases discussed here, however, engage with power in alternative ways to seek the "political sovereignty" that the Nyéléni delegates assert is a prerequisite for a more just, ecologically healthy, and fair food system.

PERMACULTURE

Permaculture is a design-based method of crop cultivation that emphasizes an ontology of integrativeness between nature and society. Key components of the permaculture system are integrated crop-livestock systems, with perennial fruit and nut trees forming the foundation of both human and animal feed. The inspiration for modern permaculture appears in European writings dating to the early twentieth century. Perhaps the most enduring treatise on permaculture is *The One-Straw Revolution*, written by Masanobu Fukuoka, who advocated for no-till orchards and rice cultivation, chemical-free farming, and crop-livestock systems in Japan in the 1930s. The contemporary form of permaculture emerged in the writings of Bill Mollison and David Holmgren in the 1970s, who worked in Tasmania to develop agricultural systems able to compete with industrial methods. Mollison has become a permaculture icon; he frequently lectures in over eighty countries and has developed a popular permaculture design course. Permaculture has since gained international attention in various media, including a popular BBC film called *A Farm for the Future*, as a form of self-reliance and a way to feed the world with minimal impact.

The core tenets of permaculture are *care for the earth*, *care for the people*, and *return of surplus*. This structure underscores horizontal symmetry between natures and cultures in which people are not bracketed off from their environments in the production of food. The idea that surplus is to be returned either to the soil in the form of compost or to people in the form of food security is a radical departure from capitalized, industrial agriculture and is a key element of permaculture's emphasis on sustainability. Permaculture works through the interconnected design of the placements of plants and animals in relationships to maximize their health and productivity. Permaculture's use of perennial crops, animals as agents in the system, and useful synergies between crops and animals as ecosystem services is also designed to minimize labor costs, decrease waste, and reduce inputs. Research on the productivity of permaculture indicates that a single acre of crops can accumulate one thousand pounds of carbon per acre-foot each year and generate 956 pounds of organic matter per year (Bates & Hemenway, 2010). The quarter-acre University of Massachusetts Permaculture Garden, which received a sustainability award from the White House in 2012, annually produces over one thousand pounds of vegetables, herbs, fruit, and berries for the dining halls. A permaculture design "food forest" also recently opened in Seattle as a collective source of free food for residents of the city (Schiller, 2013).

The Nyéléni delegates identify alternative production models as key to the success of food sovereignty. They emphasize systems that enroll eaters and farmers in "solidarity economies" in which food is produced and consumed in a way that reflects the political and ecological values of food sovereignty (i.e., soil health, democratic participation). All of the cases in this book employ some form of permaculture as production model. Some are more capitalized than others, but in general, the activists in these cases see small-scale, organic (although not certified), mixed crop-livestock and perennial plant systems as the most workable for achieving their political, social-economic, and ecological objectives. Permaculture is probably the only production model that can build a system that would restore and build soil fertility, resist privatization and enclosure, facilitate shared harvests, and confound restrictions on seed saving.

In 2010 a tribal leader at White Earth Reservation told me that some of the people who guard a spiritual community "look within, some look outside" for threats to the group. In positioning myself as someone who "looks within" and also "looks outside" for threats to food sovereignty, as both an activist and a scholar, I also refuse modernist binaries. This is informed in no small part by my own investments in food sovereignty, as a scholar, an activist, and a practitioner. As a feminist geographer, my analytical lens is simultaneously focused on the spatial, the territorial, and the intersection of the personal and the political. Toward this end, then, I bring together a critique of top-down ways of seeing, subject-object binaries, political neutrality, and objective science. In so doing, I articulate a framing of food sovereignty that is both lived and material, discursive and political. My position as a member of a variety of biosocial groups looking to bring about regime change in the food system no doubt places me in a privileged, but also partial, epistemic position, one that prioritizes intersubjective ways of knowing (McDowell, 1999).

I know food sovereignty from below, as a radical proliferation of a variety of discontents with social injustice, ecological destruction, disempowerment, and the production of hunger in the food system. While I use the feminist language of "seeing from below" and I engage in acts of "citizenship from below" through my membership in various biosocial groups, I know food sovereignty best by seeing "from within." To that end, I know and privilege food sovereignty in a particular, situated way. This is not just a personal position; it is also a political one, and I "speak with" a variety of groups advocating for collective rights to access land and share food in ways that are not criminalized.

Holt-Giménez and Shattuck (2011) warn that without alliances between groups falling at different points along the political spectrum of food sovereignty, the movement is doomed to failure or co-optation by progressive or reform trends. I argue as well that these alliances are also key to setting the terms for its engagement (if at all) with the liberal state. The ideas of radical collectivism do both material and epistemic work for food sovereignty—and work along a fault line that opens up in the literature around what role the state could or should have in achieving food security. It also makes more visible left-leaning politics in the food system and offers points of leverage and engagement across political communities within the radical trend. In what follows, I elaborate on how political autonomy and access to the commons, as articulated by the Nyéléni delegates to be central to food sovereignty, are imagined and enacted in two separate cases.

PART II

CHAPTER THREE

Temporary Commons

Urban Community Gardens

There are no gardens in the city. There are avenues, crooked streets, where
they grow the signs. But where [do] they grow lettuce, beans, turnips, radishes,
lemon . . . ?

Anonymous, Lisbon, Portugal

Across the street from a community garden in Lisbon, Portugal, above a wall
of graffiti, is written this provocative question, which confronts its reader with
the potentially uncomfortable notion that gardens as much as streets belong
in the city. The community garden next to this statement, ultimately destroyed
by the city through "development," represented material resistance to modernist notions of urban space, private property, and the appropriate place of food
production. The garden and its growers demonstrate Massey's (2005) framing
of space as something that is continuously made and remade and McKittrick's
(2006) way of thinking about space as an "interpretive alterable world" (xiii).
I present this case as a demonstration of how the urban landscape is a product
of the biopolitical power of liberal sovereignty, which ultimately has the power
to decide who or what will live (or not). But where there is power there is resistance, and the urban gardeners in this case demonstrate flexibility in their
spatial strategies to find autonomous spaces for life.

The garden at the heart of this story is literally a margin: a forgotten, mostly
hidden pocket of land carved out from a larger, older forest and garden as a
result of road construction. The gardeners live on the metaphorical margin
of society—they are elderly, immigrants, disaffected youth—claiming space
for life. The power they had, for a time, to make this space productive, came
through their and its marginality. When the land became economically valuable
as capital for the state, the garden was destroyed and remade in the image of
private property with allotments. Thus this story holds in tension social movements for rights to land from the state, or some collectively held right to control
of land as "land sovereignty" (Borras & Franco, 2012), with the power of the

FIGURE 4. The site of the former Horta do Mount after its destruction, being prepared for the Parque Horticola, July 2013. (Author's photo)

state to unilaterally seize land. The sovereign liberal state always retains the right to establish a state of exception, and it may always do so when capital comes calling. This calls into question whether the liberal state can be the guarantor of the rights food sovereignty demands, when the state's interests lie in propping up modernist notions of food production and capital accumulation.

The privatization of urban land in this story illustrates the continuation of the enclosure of land and other commons, which perpetuates the centralization of power and control of agriculture by states, supranational organizations, and corporations. Land reform, in the form of returning land to the dispossessed, is a central pillar of food sovereignty. The Nyéléni narratives stress, however, that "access," "sharing," and "rights to use" are more central than owning or (re)distributing land in the way that Borras and Franco (2012) describe as "land sovereignty." In addition, the episteme of ownership—the idea that land can be claimed, exchanged, and transferred from one person to the next—is in fact what the Nyéléni delegates say they "are fighting against." What they are "fighting for" in terms of collective land rights or usufruct rights is antithetical to capitalism and is part of what Nyers (2006) calls the "unthinkable" for the liberal state.

Urban Agriculture

Lyson (2004) identifies the geographic separation between the place of production and the place of consumption as a source of alienation between producers and consumers in modernist agriculture. One approach to closing this gap is through urban agriculture (UA) (Jarosz, 2008) and the reestablishment of local-scale food systems (Donald & Blay-Palmer, 2006). Urban agriculture seeks to reconnect producers and consumers by giving them a shared stake in the food system through "co-locating sites" of food production and consumption (Koc, MacRae, Mougeot, & Walsh, 1999; Schiavoni, 2009). The process of co-location reduces, and in many cases even erases, the distance between production and consumption and cultivates an interdependence between farmers and eaters. Minimizing the friction of distance allows the means of production to be more transparent, as opposed to obscured by the exchange of money in longer supply chains (Allen & Kovach, 2000).

Urban gardeners often see growing food in the city as deliberately political direct action and as a way to reclaim spaces and activities that have become dominated by markets. UA projects are often funded by nonprofits or subsidized by other financial sources, as they are often financially unsustainable endeavors. As such, UA, including urban livestock and community gardens, is often seen as a form of self-sufficiency and self-reliance in economic hard times. UA is increasingly popular in North American and European cities, but the slow pace of institutional change in municipalities and the bureaucratic regulatory and permitting processes hamper progress and often regulate UA initiatives out of existence.

Urban agriculture is critiqued, however, for its biases toward the "whitened cultural histories" of "good food" (Slocum, 2007; Guthman, 2008a), rather than structural problems such as economic decline, disinvestment, infrastructure abandonment, segregation, contaminated soils, and discriminatory zoning and planning. Community gardens and urban agriculture, when generated from outside the neighborhood, are often seen as paternalistic and out of touch (Guthman, 2008a). Urban agriculture projects that arise from within communities also face threats from development, (re)zoning, and gentrification. However, there are exceptions to these general trends that resonate with food sovereignty's aims to decommodify food and enact social change.

Perhaps the most compelling of such projects is the Detroit Black Farmers Community Food Security Network (DBCFSN). In the years leading up to Detroit's economic collapse in the late 2000s, the black community in the city—which is one of the most segregated cities in the United States—organized around building urban garden projects to "build community self-reliance" and "to change our consciousness about food" (DBCFSN, 2013). The network has since developed several gardens in the city in abandoned and vacant lots, created a food policy council, and fostered a cooperative buying club. In this example and many others, the power of collectively growing food produces self-reliance and alternative subjectivities as much as, or perhaps more than, the food itself (Levkoe, 2006; Winne, 2008). Urban gardens thus occupy public space to present an alternative vision of the world.

"PARKing" Days, a project of Rebar, which is based in San Francisco, are efforts to raise awareness of the ways in which public spaces in cities are appropriated for particular uses, and not others. PARKing Day activists claim a parking space by feeding the meter with the required amount of change and transform it into a garden or a park for several hours (Bishop & Williams, 2012). These actions demonstrate the productive potential of approximately 180 square feet, roughly the size of an average parking space in the United States, and reveal how a certain amount of public space is devoted to each person through the allocation of parking spots in an urban area. The right to a place to park a car is rarely challenged and usually guaranteed, often at great expense to cities and their citizens. PARKing Days work within the existing framework of individual, territorial rights to space within the city but use them to challenge normative assumptions about food production.

Inspired by PARKing Days, activists in Athens, Georgia, turned parking spaces in the downtown area into urban gardens (complete with illegal urban chickens) for a day in June 2010. The aim of this project was to change public ideas about green space in cities and to challenge ideas about the purposes to which it could be dedicated. The Athens activists chose to make their "park" a garden as a way, in the words of one activist, to "make people make the connection that the food we eat is grown somewhere; it doesn't just magically appear" (Cliff).[1] The "park" not only educates but pushes the public to question the way certain kinds of urban public space is created and used. Activists working with a similar project in Brussels, called 8m² (the metric equivalent of 180 square feet), grow food year-round in gardens on moveable carts that can be placed in parking areas. The garden is composed of raised beds on wheels that take up as much space as a parked car and are used in public to demonstrate that those who don't own a car could or should have a right to use an amount of public space the size of a parking spot for a car. The activists use these temporary installations to challenge normative assumptions about land in the city and to push toward creating, in their words, "more space for people, less for cars" (Joeren).

A form of public protest that involves growing food is known as "guerrilla gardens" (Lamborn & Weinberg, 1999), which temporarily turn urban space into gardens. Seed bombs, a tactic of guerrilla gardening, are made of a variety of biodegradable materials and are surreptitiously dropped in vacant places throughout the city in the hopes that the seeds in the "bomb" will germinate and grow. Guerrilla gardeners partner with plants to exploit the way in which municipalities exercise incomplete or partial sovereignty over space. Guerrilla gardeners, however, do their work with the full knowledge that the gardens, farms, or cultivated plots they create may be destroyed when the state or city reasserts control over the territory. This may not actually happen, given that the political usefulness of the death of plants may not be worth that expenditure of resources. The assumed and widely accepted temporality of these installations reveals something about the municipality's partial control of its territory and the spaces that margins provide for political action.

FIGURE 5. 8m² gardens, Brussels, Belgium. (Author's photo)

Commons

The enclosure of agricultural land sowed the seeds for the modernization and commoditization of agriculture. The land base supporting a precapitalist agriculture was traditionally a shared resource, held in the form of what we now call the "commons." Enclosure had the effect of privatizing land, as well as separating farmers from relations of interdependence on each other. The destruction of the commons as a mode of production allowed for the rationalization of agriculture to proceed, one farmer at a time. According to van der Ploeg (2010), enclosure and subsequent industrialization of agriculture contributed to land losing its importance and relevance as ecological capital. Land, as the commons, had historically been the resource base that made agricultural production possible and to which farmers contributed collectively as a means of building ecological capital. Land is now simply seen as the staging area for the conversion of commodities into other commodities, which in theory could happen anywhere (van der Ploeg, 2010).

Historically, the commons have been collectively held resources, most of them natural, but also social, and they continue to include things like water or the atmosphere. Water, for example, is still held collectively largely because it cannot yet be reasonably privatized or "enclosed." When an individual or group asserts a claim to ownership over a historically shared resource, it is effectively privatized, unless use rights are granted to those who do not own the resource. A successfully managed commons provides a number of measurable outcomes, including the development of alternative forms of exchange, collective action, and equitable sharing of resources (Agarwal, 2014). While the benefits of the commons should not be overstated, the management of common-pool resources is a contested project (Agarwal, 2014) and one not well suited to the way liberal democracies govern people and things. Elinor Ostrom (1990), probably the most widely recognized expert on the commons, asserts that "polycentric" models of governance—in which local, informal management is supported by actors at multiple scales, including the state—are key to managing and maintaining the commons. What should be avoided, in Ostrom's estimation, are the very structures that characterize governance of common-pool resources in liberal democracies: property regimes that favor some form of enclosure and centralized control, usually through government agencies (Pennington, 2012).

In the Nyéléni declaration, the delegates assert what they are fighting against in very clear terms: "Around the world we confront government policies which promote industrial agriculture through *privatization of commons* such as water, land, and seas" (2007: 45, emphasis added). Land reform has thus been a key platform from which food sovereigntists claim rights to space and territory for food production. Delegates demand agrarian reform that ensures peasant "priority in the use of land, water, seeds and livestock breeds" and in which "customary rights to territory must be recognized," and they "promote community-based management of territories" (Nyéléni, 2007: 56). Unfortunately, current land reform efforts redistribute publicly held lands into private ownership—in what appears to be an ongoing process of enclosing the commons (Borras & Franco, 2012).

Struggles against this process include the assertion of "political control over remaining lands against potential and actual threats . . . via community-based enclosure of the commons" (Borras & Franco, 2012: 9). Borras and Franco call this a people's counter-enclosure, which can include the pooling of resources, such as land held under community control, while granting use rights to the community. This is a critical piece of shifting the balance backward, toward noncommoditized modes of production. Shared ecological capital, for which no one pays rent, is the foundation of a noncommoditized food system. To reclaim the commons in the context of the liberal sovereign state is paradoxical, however, unless new modes of governance can also be realized within the state.

Territory and the Temporary Commons

Underpinning the concept of sovereignty is the mutual exclusivity of claims to space; modernist state sovereignty is not characterized by multiple or overlapping claims to one territory. Transnational and supranational political shifts may be changing this, however, in the construction of new geographies of power and sovereignty over space (Agnew, 2005; Anderson, 1996; Appadurai, 2003; Simpson, 2014). Indeed, Anderson (1996) suggests that the postmodern unbundling of social life from territorial states constitutes a shift forward or back to what he calls "medieval territorialities" (134). This new medievalism is characterized by overlapping authorities (and associated allegiances) similar to those that governed different aspects of social, political, and economic life before the rise of the modern nation-state. Similarly, Appadurai (2003) suggests that the postnational world is characterized by "transecting maps of allegiance and a politics of non-exclusive, territorial copresence" (343).

Elden (2010) describes territory as a technology of power in which space is produced by the state as a way to measure and control the population and the resources within its bounds. Territorial formations are thus a geographical expression of power upon which the state hopes and intends to make a permanent claim. Storey (2001), however, suggests that territory is always and already a temporary spatial strategy as competing interests continue to (re)appropriate space over time. An example of territory mobilized to challenge state sovereignty is the temporary autonomous zone (TAZ) (Bey, 2003; Bishop & Williams, 2012). Also known as "freezones," TAZs offer a space of bounded autonomy for dissidents and free thinkers and often operate at the political and economic margins of the state for the purposes of allowing nonnormative political discourses and practices to be realized (Bey, 2003). These spaces are often strongly associated with anarchist politics but are animated by discourses of action that move away from state overthrow and toward creating spaces of freedom, self-reliance, and mutual aid (Bishop & Williams, 2012) beyond the biopolitical control of the state but within its territorial bounds. These actors often mobilize the weapons of the weak in the form of noncompliance, passive resistance, and nonparticipation (Scott, 2008).

The fiction of the territorial nation-state as a fixed, mutually exclusive space is challenged and replaced in some imaginaries as a series of spaces knit together by the identities and allegiances of those who inhabit those spaces (Simpson, 2014). According to Appadurai (2003), identities and allegiances between and among social groups are now more powerful than the territorial state in shaping political affiliations, and rights associated with territory are sometimes extended beyond the bounds of the state. The territory of India, for example, is copresent in the United States through special economic rights given to those of Indian nationality living outside of India. Appadurai suggests that social movements, operationalized from this way of thinking about space, can support a reterritorialization of space based on an "imaginary of local autonomy" in a deterritorialized state. He writes that these are "exercises in the creation of new local imaginaries, relatively free from the discourses of patriotism and nationality but rich in the discourses of citizenship, democracy and local rights" (345).

These ideas resonate with what Hardt and Negri (2009) call the "multitude." The multitude is composed of people who organize against "traditional, organizational forms based on unity, central leadership, and hierarchy [which] are neither desirable, nor effective" (166). Hardt and Negri link the political possibilities of the multitude to its basis in mutualist, as opposed to privatized, notions of shared resources: "The becoming political of the multitude does not require leaving behind the state of nature, as the tradition of sovereignty insists, but rather calls for a metamorphosis of the common that operates simultaneously on nature, culture, and society" (171).

The commons constitutes the sum total of social and natural resources that could, theoretically, be available to all residents of the planet, including biopolitical capital such as air, water, and soil and social capital belonging to language, knowledge, and tradition (Ostrom, 1990). In their treatment of the "making of the multitude," Hardt and Negri (2009) assert, following Žižek (2006), that radical or revolutionary subjects will not emerge from within the structures that dominate them. They argue instead, following Foucault, that the emergence of revolutionary subjects is constitutive of the struggle for power itself. Thus the act of resistance to authority creates the revolutionary subject, and Hardt and Negri (2009) urge us to "intervene in the circuits of the production of subjectivity, free from the apparatuses of control, and construct the bases for an autonomous production" (172).

If state-capital sovereignty over territory is seen as only a partial and temporary strategy, the resulting peeling back of the fiction of totalizing state power opens up possibilities for overlapping—spatially and temporally—sovereignties. These potentially subversive political uses of space appeal to neither the state nor capital for solutions and instead rely on spaces of bounded autonomy in the margins. These spaces allow for dissent and a refusal to participate in "statism," and they foster the "unthinkable" in the form of self-sufficiency and mutualist forms of relations. These contested struggles for autonomy might function as a kind of oppositional "state of exception" against the biopolitical control of the state—even if only temporarily. The garden described below became a temporary space of autonomy through the gardeners' refusal to enclose the commons and consent to modernist urban values and development.

Horta do Mount: Temporary Commons

During the spring of 2007, in Lisbon, Portugal, permaculture activists planted a community garden in an empty and ambiguously zoned space with a breathtaking view of the Atlantic Ocean. The garden was in a rapidly gentrifying neighborhood of Lisbon, one that tourists frequent because of its view and historical significance as one of the oldest settled areas of the city. The activists claim that they built the garden to accommodate desires for an urban garden in the

FIGURE 6. Sign at the Horta do Mount garden entrance, 2010. (Author's photo)

neighborhood and that they began with the city's permission—although that is contested now. The garden is situated between a South Asian immigrant community, a neighborhood of retirees, and a more upscale area popular with young people. Many of the original gardeners came from these neighborhoods, but most were forced out due to rapidly rising rents. The garden was established on "unused" and abandoned municipal land that had once been part of a city park, and before that was part of a large garden around a convent. Before the garden was established, the land, according to the gardeners, was used by nearby residents to "dump garbage and walk the dog."

Lisbon has a tradition, referred to as *baldio*, of using vacant land for pasturing animals. These parcels are very much like "commons" in other places and hold a particular, if ambiguous, kind of zoning status within the city. Many, including the gardeners, believed that the garden was *baldio*, but in fact the piece of land in question (inside circle, upper left-hand corner, figure 7) was part of Convent De Graca, which included a church and a large food garden with trees and shrubs. The Horta do Mount garden was cut off from the rest of the garden by the construction of a street sometime before 1994. The convent and grounds were made a Portuguese national monument in 1910 and held in trust by the army as a base for a variety of its operations until 2012, when it transferred the buildings and grounds to the city of Lisbon.

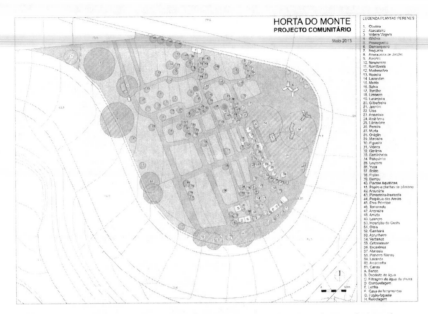

FIGURE 7. Record of plant species in the Horta do Mount garden, 2013. (Horta du Monde, used with permission)

A group of Lisbon residents affiliated with the larger-scale organization GAIA planted the original garden at the site in 2007. GAIA is an international organization that focuses on social justice and environmental issues, specifically those relating to ecological debt between the Global North and South. GAIA's local chapter in Lisbon held community suppers and hosted educational events about ecological debt and sustainable living. In 2010 the group associated with GAIA handed over responsibility and daily maintenance work in the garden to a group calling themselves Horta do Mount. According to their website, the Horta do Mount is "a community project aimed at promoting healthier lifestyles and sustainable towns, through the practice of organic farming according to the principles of permaculture, creating and strengthening ties between people of different age groups, where sharing and knowledge transfer happen" (Horta do Monte, n.d.).

The Horta do Mount Community Project develops activities according to three specific objectives, which are consistent with food sovereignty and urban agriculture projects: participation in collective food production, education for sustainability, and the promotion of human and ecological health. The garden was a critical space for the mission of Horta do Mount because it provided a space to work toward all three of those objectives.

By 2013 the Horta do Mount garden was home to sixty useful plant species, most of them perennial shrubs and trees. It was a notable site of social inclusion, transgressing many social divisions, and was open to all, literally. There was no fence or gate, and a sign at the entrance of the garden saying "participa" encouraged anyone to get involved. No single person had an individual plot (or allotment), and the planting, maintenance, and harvest were a collective effort by anyone who wanted to participate. Inez, an activist for the garden, said in an interview, "We made the garden open to everyone on purpose." Echoing Inez and invoking a populist vision of the commons, Pedro simply stated, "When a tree is planted by the community, it is to the community."

The garden was a site for educational activities, including classes on permaculture, solar technologies, and healthy living. According to the activists, in its first three years alone, the project involved as gardeners, activists, and students more than three hundred people from a variety of walks of life, including elderly, retired, and unemployed members of the community. In 2013 the garden partnered with an organization called the Art of Living, which conducted educational courses in the garden. This group also hosted community suppers each week, which involved cooking and eating Ayurvedic vegetarian food in a shared community space. When I asked Pedro what he meant by community, he answered broadly, but he also spoke of its effect specifically on the neighborhood: "The community is everyone. Anyone who wants to be involved. Anyone who benefits from trees being planted. Which is basically all of us. But we had old and young people, residents and immigrants, men and women, employed and unemployed. The garden was especially important for the unemployed because they have something to do all day besides stay at home and watch TV. They get outside and do something important and fulfilling. They loved the garden."

While the gardeners and activists generally articulate a sense of the commons as essential for permaculture and the kind of community they aim to foster, Gil was the most resolute in his stance, saying, "I don't believe in private property" when asked why they made the garden open to all. The gardeners are also individually linked to the larger transition town movement, which promotes permaculture as a mode of production. Their affiliation with various organizations promoting permaculture not only lent them skills to develop the garden but also provided the context for sustainable agroecological practices and philosophies to proliferate at the site. According to Carla, the purpose of the garden was built on the permaculture principles of "care for people, care for land, growing and sharing."

In addition to fostering openness and the growing of perennial plants such as trees, permaculture ideas also influenced the choices the gardeners made about irrigation. The garden always had a tenuous water supply, granted at the whim of city officials through neighborhood fire hydrants. It was often turned off capriciously, according to some of the gardeners. According to Pedro, the water also was a source of unsustainability for the garden: "The water supply to Lisbon comes from three hundred miles away. It's not sustainable. Our water supply with the ollas irrigation system was. We made it that way." Tired of the unreliability and unsustainability of their water source, in 2013 the gardeners constructed a sophisticated but low-tech rainwater harvesting and irrigation system using all renewable materials.[2] One gardener, describing the now destroyed garden in a very emotional interview, said, "We were just trying to be sustainable. It was a multifunctional garden. It had habitat for pollinators and other animals. We grew medicinal plants. We had bees." Saying this, she paused, wiped tears, and said again, her voice shaking, "We had bees" (Inez).

State of Exception

In 2013 the Horta do Mount garden was demolished by the city of Lisbon and replaced with privatized garden allotments for which gardeners will pay a fee. The destruction involved occupation by municipal police and the use of industrial-scale excavation equipment to remove all the trees. They also removed and destroyed buildings housing a community seed bank and tools, artwork, irrigation structures, and educational materials. According to the activists, they were not given notice of the removal until the morning of the destruction. Public officials say the activists were involved in two meetings at which the removal of the garden was discussed. In any case, there was no public comment period, and police without badges or IDs prevented the activists from interfering in the destruction. They also detained protestors and confiscated cameras to erase images of the destruction. Charges were not pressed against the activists, and the judge dismissed their cases.

When I visited the garden in 2013, the space had been cleared and was under construction as part of a "horticulture park" associated with the convent and its associated gardens. It is rumored that the convent will become a luxury hotel, like other such private developments in Lisbon. The horticultural park is a project spearheaded by the city as part of a larger plan for green space and urban gardens. In the first comprehensive land use plan developed by the city, for 1994–2012, the garden was designated "nonstructured green space" by the city. It had no identifiable owner, but this is not terribly unusual in a city as old as Lisbon, where land may never have been entered into formal title. As Jao explained, "No one knows who owns what in this town. It's a huge problem for development because projects languish for years as people try to figure out who owns a piece of property." The ambiguous legal status of the garden made it an ideal site for the gardeners' purposes, however. "It was not clearly defined as any particular kind of space, so it was open for anyone to get involved" (Pedro).

As justification for the garden's destruction, the municipal council argued that the permaculture garden was an eyesore and disliked by the community around it. They also said the neighborhood had circulated a petition to have it removed. The activists disagree, saying the petition was misleading and not directed at their garden. In any case, competing visions of what a garden is and does and how it should look are at the root of the conflict between the gardeners, the community, and the city. One of the council member's employees identified the garden as dirty and disorganized in his personal blog. He referred to the removal of the garden as "limpeza" (cleaning) and said that the garden was a "dumpster" that had no productive plants (Mata, 2013).

The activists argue that their initial vision for the space was not well supported by the city when they began. Inez said, "From the beginning, they were not on board with our vision for the garden. They wanted a conventional urban garden with allotments. We were trying to do something different by keeping it open and making it by the community, to the community. They have never understood this, and in our attempts to talk to them since the first meeting, they have treated us like we *didn't even exist.*"

In the end, the city exerted its authority over the space and enclosed it without much in the way of consent from the community near it, the general public, or the gardeners. The activists argue that the garden was always threatened and that the city would occasionally turn off the water supply to the garden and did so a few weeks before the removal. The gardeners also suspected that their planting of trees interfered with the city's long-term economic development plans for the site, given that full-grown trees would be difficult and expensive to remove. The gardeners asserted, "They wanted to take control of the space. They did that by removing everything we had planted without our permission and then asking us to come back under the new rules" (Jao).

The new rules for the garden space include an allotment system for garden space that requires payment, privatizing something that had been open, public, and democratically controlled. The city also requires that any gardener agree to leave when given notice, thus retaining ultimate control over the space, the life in the garden, and the people who wish to garden in it. The city also stipulates that no trees may be planted, effectively rendering permaculture designs impossible to implement. These rules exist for other urban gardens that are managed by the city in its comprehensive plan for urban green space. The modernist economic function of space in the city is upheld by these new rules, effectively forcing people off collectively worked land and into capitalist relations with the city-state.

This plan is consistent with the modernist vision of urban green space that is tightly controlled by municipal authorities, rendering life subject to the biopolitical control of a sovereign government. After the destruction of the garden, the Horta do Mount gardeners quickly moved to a new site, the location of which was kept confidential by the gardeners and the organizations of which they are a part until it was established. They say they are building Horta du Monde (garden for the world). According to one activist, the destruction of Horta do Mount created an opportunity for positive change—it "let the garden

grow wings" (Carla). As such, the gardeners view space as always open to altera-
tion, believing that the commons can be (re)generated—even if only temporarily—in many spaces. Rather than making a permanent claim to territory, the
activists exert a temporary claim over ambiguously territorialized space, thus
operationalizing an understanding of variegated sovereignty. They also articulate and practice a collective—but ultimately condemned—notion of property.

This spatial strategy does not require a fixed space, only an available space.
In many instances, the more flexible and ambiguous the space, the better. Formal arrangements through property rights or other codified relationships that
involve regulation often make space exclusive to those with the capital to access
it. Thus open, ambiguous, unproductive space used on a temporary basis is an
effective tool for those without other forms of power. This strategy becomes a
"weapon of the weak," used from the margins in a biopolitical struggle over
what can live and what must die. In this case, the city exerted its power over
space through a violent act of exception, but the strategy of resistance and engagement with this power was to move the garden to another place, effectively
continuing to exploit the partial and incomplete control that the city holds over
its own territory.

If all social struggles are spatial, then changing the terrain on which a struggle
is engaged necessarily changes the outcomes of the struggle (Martin & Miller,
2003). Activists in the cases discussed in this chapter changed the terrain of
struggle over decision making in the food system by territorializing unused
open space rather than making claims against the state for rights. Gardeners
in these examples call upon mutualist notions of property to create a food-
producing garden and are allowed, for a time, to "self-rule." Because urban gardens, particularly those inspired by food sovereignty, are almost always threatened by development of many kinds, the strategy often invoked is to *temporarily*
territorialize space as a political strategy to subvert the power of the city or state.
The ambiguous and ultimately temporary nature of these gardens allowed this
strategy of mutualist direct action to flourish for a time without much attention
from the biopolitical control of city or state. The city ultimately exercised its
power over each of the spaces, but the strategies of temporariness and marginality used by the activists demonstrate useful and instructive responses to
assertions of power in the interests of capital on the part of the state.

Using the examples of displaced persons, Appadurai (2003) illustrates a postnational geography of power by describing how communities in transit reterritorialize space through the appropriation of resources in a particular place.
Denying access to productive resources is a strategy of the biopower of the
modernist state, and displaced persons often must siphon resources off from
legitimate structures in quasilegal ways. Food sovereigntists also reterritorialize
space and appropriate resources without permission from the state, and they

can be seen as displaced persons in food systems governed by regulations of the nation-state that uphold and defend monopolies of power over life in the food system. Food sovereigntists thus mobilize territory as a partial and temporary technology of power (Elden, 2010) to shift the scale and locus of power from the nation or the city to local affiliations. Through the quasilegal appropriation of resources, actors in these imaginaries are also partially and temporarily freed from the state's legal apparatus governing the territorial space that they inhabit. They are able to create a temporary zone of autonomy, or a "sovereignty within sovereignty" (Simpson, 2014: 10).

The Horta do Mount activists, through their permaculture gardens, created a temporary commons as part a biopolitical struggle with the city for power. While this is not a classic, nor even a good, example of food sovereignty, resistance to modernist notions of urban space through agroecological and mutualist social relations signal a lived engagement with Hardt and Negri's (2009) "multitude" or "radical collectivism." This is key to the wider food sovereignty struggle, as it legitimates permaculture as a mode of food production, mutualist notions of property through the commons, and self-governance through openness and inclusion "by making it by the community, for the community." Mutualism and agroecology, however, are tolerated only as long as they do not interfere with the accumulation of capital. What is more important than the practice of food sovereignty in this case, and what it best demonstrates, is that the actions of the city constituted a "state of exception" in which the city exercised its power over territory to acquire capital for private development. To protect and preserve the commons and mutualism against a state of exception, then, requires an alternative mode of governance that conceptualizes the rights of nature and communities in radically different ways, which is the subject of the next chapter.

CHAPTER FOUR

Spatial Practices of Governance

Community-Based Rights

When we asserted our right to self-governance of our food system in our towns in
Maine, we are fundamentally, foundationally, going back to our roots. We reject
the right of governmental agencies to define us or what we do in a way that
undermines our safety and happiness.

Heather Retberg, "The New Radical: Going Back to Our Agricultural Roots," 2012

In the spring of 2011, several townships in Hancock County, Maine, passed a
Community Self-Governance Ordinance as part of the town meeting cycle that
characterizes home rule governance (see the appendix for the full text of the
ordinance). The ordinance was largely a response to changes to key state laws
governing food safety that would negatively affect many small-scale farmers.
Inspired by the work of the Community Environmental Legal Defense Fund
(CELDF), the ordinance aimed to protect the rights of residents to produce and
consume foods of their choosing by exempting them from state law through
self-governance. Several farmers, acting on the belief that the ordinance protected their activities, continued to operate their businesses as usual. The ordinances have since been found by the courts to be illegitimate assertions of
authority and the farmers have subsequently been arrested, fined, and sued
(Bangor Daily News, 2011; Berleant, 2013). The food sovereignty ordinances
define the rights of citizens to shape the rules governing food production by
prohibiting limits to those rights. These efforts to establish autonomy and
self-governance for small-scale agriculture were then reframed as a criminal
de/re-territorializing of sovereign state space (Kurtz, 2013).

The rule change in 2009 in Maine primarily affected small-scale poultry producers, many of whom also produce and market other meat, eggs, and dairy.
Among those who thought their food production and distribution practices
were protected by the ordinances was Dan Brown, who owned and operated a
small-scale diversified farming operation with one milk cow. Brown had sold
raw milk in several local markets for many years, but in 2011 he was told he

needed to acquire a license to sell his milk or change his marketing strategy. Although he complied with the requirements, the target was a moving one, and Brown was repeatedly found in violation of state and federal laws. The Department of Agriculture filed a suit against Brown, who sought protection under home rule and the "Food Sovereignty Ordinance" passed in Blue Hill. The judge ruled against him, arguing that "raw milk" was not covered under the ordinance.

The changes to the Maine agricultural rules foreshadowed sweeping new federal regulation in the Food Safety and Modernization Act, signed into law in 2011. Widespread outrage at the way the FSMA provided few exemptions for small-scale farmers in its stringent food safety standards, which would require capital-intensive investments, affordable by only the largest-scale farmers, prompted a prolonged comment period. Farmers and their supporters were concerned that complying with the rules would be too expensive for small-scale farmers and that the FSMA was biased toward large-scale industrial models of agriculture. The law thus codifies industrial-scale farms and processors as the only legal model for production and distribution of food. In this way, policy becomes the vehicle for the interests of corporate capital to assert its dominance in the food system. The Maine food sovereignty ordinances challenged this dominance but failed to protect and implement their vision of autonomy, for reasons that this chapter details.

In this chapter I assert that under U.S. law, corporate rights, the right of the liberal state to govern, and the primacy of private property all support a regime of rights and power in favor of capital. The state's right to govern trumps the rights of local communities to govern, particularly with respect to trade and exchange both across state lines and within local communities. The development of local economies that the Nyéléni delegates advocate for thus risks failure by "capture" in the legal apparatus of the liberal sovereign state, as demonstrated by Brown's case. On the other hand, food sovereignty, as political sovereignty, troubles some of the key assumptions of the liberal state. In many ways the actions toward community self-governance in the food sovereignty ordinances elaborate on and enact a different kind of state sovereignty and recast the relationship between citizens and their state in new ways.

Local Food Systems

Local food systems have always existed in both rural and urban spaces. They diminished in significance in the middle of the twentieth century as agriculture modernized in the United States but persisted in informal ways from the 1950s onward. Local food lived on in the sales of surplus eggs from backyard hens, the purchase of a side of beef from a neighbor, the tapping of a dairy farmer's bulk tank, and the clandestine deposit of a surfeit of zucchini on a neighbor's porch. In the 1990s the informal market in local produce, dairy, eggs, and meat became marketable as consumers became increasingly uneasy about the sources of their food (Trauger, 2004). The emergence of organic farmers in the 1980s and organic's widespread adoption as a federal program in the 2000s signaled a rejection of modernist agriculture on the part of both the producer and the consumer and marked a transition to a new agricultural economy. Organic production as a technical practice, however, was easily inserted into the globalization of food, and now one can buy organic and Fair Trade commodities from nearly anywhere in the world.[1] Rather than bringing social and environmental justice, the transformation of small-scale farm products into global commodities through their certification as organic or Fair Trade have only made them "safe for capitalism" (Guthman, 1998: 150).

The organic movement identified the codification of standards as part of its struggle for legitimacy and market share, but the implementation of standards, both nationally and globally, has considerably watered them down (Trauger & Murphy, 2013). The involvement of the USDA and other global regulatory agencies has reduced the organic standards to extensive checklists, expensive practices, and time-consuming paperwork that are easily met by large-scale producers, who now dominate the market. Small-scale farmers have dropped their certifications in favor of capitalizing on a comparative advantage in local markets. Certified Naturally Grown, an alternative certification, is growing in popularity with growers, as are more informal mechanisms such as community supported agriculture (Harrison, 2008). The codification of organic, far from protecting small-scale farmers, has actually led to their increased marginalization. The regulation of organic agriculture became a pathway upon which operators of large-scale farms and multinational corporations seized an advantage.

Given this history and backdrop, small-scale producers are concerned about what the implementation of the FSMA might mean for their operations, particularly those who operate mixed vegetable and livestock farms and use composted manure from their own animals as fertilizer. The FSMA was created in response to a spate of increasingly widespread and lethal outbreaks of food-borne illnesses, as well as post-9/11 concerns about the security of the food system. It has been widely reported that the FSMA aims to shift the FDA's efforts away from simply responding to contamination after it happens to preventing it from occurring in the first place. Allegedly, because so many food-borne illnesses are linked to pathogens harbored by animals, the new rules focus on segregating animals and their wastes from places of food production, such as vegetable plots. The proposed rules would also criminalize many of the organic and sustainable techniques that many small-scale farmers have worked for decades to perfect (Halper, 2014). Techniques such as composting animal manures prioritize closing loops and minimize purchased inputs as both environmental best practices and economic strategies to cut costs. The rules will also prohibit the cultivation of land with livestock, an important source of nonpetroleum-based fertilizer, non-fossil-fuel work energy, and pest control.

The concern for small-scale farmers who primarily sell into local markets is that the rules assume an unfair "one-size-fits-all" approach to governance of the food system. According to Almy (2013), activism for local control reflects fears that FSMA regulations are "tailored toward facilitating large-scale food production at the expense of the family farm and traditional agricultural values" (796). Opponents of the rules argue that the rule makers are out of touch and will drive small-scale farmers out of business. Jim Crawford, a well-known pioneer in sustainable agriculture and founder of a regional cooperative in Pennsylvania, suggests that the rules may force many small-scale farmers out of business. He says, "The public loves to love and idealize us little family farmers. But the vast majority of us are hanging by a thread. Now, the government is saying, 'We are going to put a lot more weight on that thread'" (quoted in Halper, 2014).[2]

Rights to Govern and the State

The Nyéléni documents appeal to states for changes to policies and the implementation of new policies to protect the interests of smallholders and communities in a protectionist regulatory strategy. While the politicization of the food system via food sovereignty is clearly about changing the nature of decision making about food distribution and production, and many scholars acknowledge this (Patel, 2009; Claeys, 2012; Desmarais & Wittman, 2014), a reformist social movement strategy is often inadequate to counter the economic agenda of the liberal state. National states reserve the right to regulate all trade, and liberal sovereignty is premised on the primacy of private property and individual rights. Thus, in the context of the liberal state, small-scale farmers and communities must grapple with laws that support the rights of corporations and the rights of the state to govern as part of the social contract. In the United States, the Commerce Clause of the Constitution, which establishes the supremacy of the federal government over states and cities, exists to effectively preempt local governance of trade. This is a key challenge to the food sovereignty strategy of appealing to the state for rights, because the privileging of capital that made the state the problem must first be changed if the state is to provide an avenue for the solution.

SOVEREIGNTY AND GOVERNING

Food-regime theorists argue that the state is subordinated to transnational capital (Friedmann, 1980). Others argue that the state is produced through a struggle for power between civil society, social movements, and transnational capital (Otero, 2012). As such, the policies that govern the food system can be seen to result from the contestation between transnational capital in the interests of profit and social movements in those of small farmers or consumers, in a Polanyian double movement between (neo)liberal and protectionist policies (Holt-Giménez & Shattuck, 2011). Alkon and Mares (2012) argue that previous food movements such as food justice have failed because they have neglected to attend to the way the corporate food regime works through policies that enable its power. Food sovereignty offers some hope for radical reform, but only if it can tackle the way liberal sovereignty produces particular kinds of social relations and subjectivities that further its ends (McCarthy & Prudham, 2004).

The territorial nation-state establishes sovereignty over people, space, and transactions as an emergent property of social relations within and between states, as well as through repeated performances of normative notions of citizenship and belonging that support the economy of the state. The shift from territorial rule under a sovereign to one shaped through relations of governing also signaled the shift from the economy as one of the family to one of the state. "The transition which takes place in the eighteenth century from an art of government to a political science, from a regime dominated by structures of sovereignty to one ruled by techniques of government, turns on the theme of population and hence also on the birth of political economy" (Foucault, 1991: 101).

Foucault—in his essay "Governmentality"—does not elaborate on what kind of economy can or should be produced through these relations of power and subjection, but he does indicate that the state and its economy are sites of struggle, both internal and external to the state's territory and governance structures. The state, to develop its economy, must form some kind of paternalistic property control and territorial boundedness modeled on patriarchal social relations. Foucault (1991) writes, "To govern a state will therefore mean to apply economy, to set up an economy at the level of the entire state, which means exercising towards its inhabitants and the wealth and behavior of each and all, a form of surveillance and control as attentive as that of the head of a family over his household and his goods" (92).

The framing of state sovereignty as produced through, and productive of, the economy overturns "the false dichotomies between state and market" and emphasizes "the proliferation and diffusion of state power through multiple institutional forms" (McCarthy & Prudham, 2004: 280). It is also instructive for understanding how the transnational food regime works.

According to Heynen, McCarthy, Prudham, and Robbins (2007), neoliberalism has as its central imperative "to expand opportunities for capital investment and accumulation by reworking state-market-civil society relationships to allow for the stretching and deepening of commodity production, circulation and exchange" (10). While neoliberal apologists shroud it in the rhetoric of freedom from government intervention in the economy, they also work to reform policies to further capital investment and circulation. Hardly laissez-faire, neoliberalism enables the development of a set of policies and regulatory apparatuses that facilitate capital accumulation rather than free capital from regulation. Given this context, can neoliberal citizen-subjects ever resist or evade the disciplinary power of the state?

Cadman (2010) engages with Foucault's work on "how not to be governed" and argues that practices Foucault terms "counter-conducts" are essential, rather than antithetical, to the practice of governmentality. Counter-conducts that advance rights as claims against the state (such as freedom from unreasonable searches and seizures) are part of the creative, "active and performative" process of governing. Cadman asserts that rights both act as powerful disciplinary tools for neoliberal governance, when mobilized through liberal notions of freedom, and also serve as a key platform from which to launch campaigns that question governments. Cadman's thesis rests on the observation that "neither governors nor governed act directly on each other; instead they act on the transactional field or domain through which they are engaged" (550). She argues that "those who are governed, and who are free to act, not only have the right to question the actions of government, but can also intervene when governments themselves fail to act" (553). The right to self-govern is the inevitable and perhaps ultimate right when governments fail to act.

COMMERCE CLAUSE

In the United States, the Constitution arose from a need for a centralized authority granting powers of supremacy over the newly formed subnational states. The Commerce Clause (article I, section 8, clause 3) describes one of the powers granted to Congress in the Constitution, which is to "regulate commerce with foreign Nations, and among the several States and with the Indian [*sic*] tribes." This clause effectively provides federal authority to govern all economic affairs within the United States as well as with other national states. The degree to which the federal government is involved in economic matters between groups has varied over time according to the way the Supreme Court has interpreted these powers. Under decisions issued in the early twentieth century in response to challenges to the Commerce Clause, Congress has been given the power to regulate and to "protect and advance" interstate commerce, in order to "prevent interstate trade from being destroyed or impeded by the rivalries of local governments" (Shreveport Rate Cases, 1914). When this is the law of the land, trade that is not sanctioned by the federal government is outlawed, and the federal right to sanction trade trumps all other rights, with few exceptions.

That the federal government would protect its right to regulate and ban interstate commerce over people's right to food was made clear in a recent case involving the transport of raw milk into Georgia from South Carolina. The case was brought by the Farm-to-Consumer Legal Defense Fund (FTCLDF) against the FDA for its attempt to criminalize the sale of raw milk across state lines. Unpasteurized milk is legal to produce and sell to customers in South Carolina, but not to people who live in Georgia. Thus, consumers in Georgia sought to purchase it outside the state, which according to the FDA violates the Commerce Clause. The case against the FDA was thrown out on technical grounds, but not before lawyers for the FDA elaborated on the "right to food" versus the right of the federal government to regulate commerce. They argued that "substantive due process does not protect, or even recognize, rights to foods of one's choosing or rights to physical health, and . . . extending constitutional protection to such rights would place the matter outside the arena of public debate and legislative action" (Kurtz, Trauger, & Passidomo, 2013: 142). In short, the rights to food that the plaintiffs asserted as fundamental to their health and well-being were considered secondary to the interests of government to regulate, promote, and protect trade.

The protections of the state's right to govern trade extend to protecting the interests of corporate capital. The rights of corporations to be treated as citizen subjects have existed since at least 1819, with the case of *Trustees of Dartmouth College v. Woodward* (17 U.S. 518), which established that private charters, or contracts between private individuals and private property, were inviolable by the state. This is widely viewed as establishing a legal basis for American corporations and the system of private enterprise in the United States. The ruling in *Pembina Consolidated Silver Mining Co. v. Pennsylvania* (125 U.S. 181) in 1888 upheld the rights of corporations under the Fourteenth Amendment and thus established them as equivalent to persons under the law. The judgment identified corporations as "associations of individuals" and, significantly, held that incorporation in multiple states (and therefore engagement in interstate commerce) does not violate the Commerce Clause, effectively giving corporations the same rights as individuals and more autonomy than local governments under federal laws regulating trade. Theoretically, any appeal by local communities or farmers to the national state for rights to govern trade at a local scale is antithetical to the reasons for the liberal state to exist, but food sovereignty activists see an opening for change in the possibilities that home rule offers municipalities.

FEDERALISM AND DEMOCRACY

Under municipal governance in England, and later in the United States, towns were originally granted a degree of autonomy from centralized authority (i.e., the king) through the development of municipal economies and tax revenues (Bower, 1985). Protections granted to landed nobility by the king created a legal relationship between central and local authority that eventually turned municipalities into a "revocable franchise" chartered by the central authority. Unless expressly authorized by its charter, any municipality that engaged in activities counter to central authority would be considered to have stepped outside the law. This concept of municipal power, known as Dillon's Rule, became the norm for chartering local authorities in the United States. The powers of a municipality to govern derived only from that which was expressly written in its charter.

The idea was to protect the municipality from both state legislatures and corrupt local authorities, but critics argue that this rule was used as a tool to legally promote the interests of corporations. According to U.S. Circuit Court justice John Dillon, in a widely referenced ruling in 1868, "Municipal corporations owe their origin to, and derive their powers and rights wholly from, the legislature. It breathes into them the breath of life, without which they cannot exist. As it creates, so may it destroy. If it may destroy, it may abridge and control" (*Clinton v. Cedar Rapids and the Missouri River Railroad*, 1868). The decision in this case prevented cities in Iowa from intervening in decisions made by the state government about placement of railroad lines. Critics of Dillon's Rule argue that it undermines all democratic rights to local self-governance and removes any kind of legal legitimacy from municipal authorities.

The alternative to Dillon's Rule is home rule, which in theory grants self-governing powers to administrative units within the bounds of a state's territory. In general, these powers extend only to those decisions that have been decentralized from the state government, and as such, as under Dillon's Rule, the municipality must first be granted the authority to make rules. Home rule municipal charters may also be abolished by state government if this power is granted within the state's constitution and laws. Even within home rule states, the law of express or implied preemption can trump the actions of local government (Diller, 2007). According to Almy (2013), home rule "grants municipalities a plenary power to function not expressly or implicitly denied by the legislature" (795). Thus, so long as not expressly or implicitly prohibited from doing so, a municipality is "free to act to promote the well-being of its citizens" (795).

Express preemption occurs when state power is expressly articulated, while implied preemption is subject to interpretation in the courts. Because implied preemption can be somewhat ambiguous (compared to express preemption), "implied pre-emption is the battleground for decision-making authority [in] home rule regimes" (Diller, 2007: 1127). Thus the difference between these two systems is not necessarily whether one does or does not have the right of self-government but rather whether a state government is more or less willing to grant rights of self-governance. In general, home rule grants municipalities authority over anything not expressly prohibited by the Constitution and over that which their charter gives them authority. In matters of commerce, national state governments are unwilling to grant subnational states or municipalities any kind of power over transactions.

The Maine self-governance ordinances are just one example of pushback against federal authority, however. Radical and critical social movements, according to Holston (1998), assert that the state is not the "only legitimate source of citizenship rights, meanings and practices" (39). Critical social movements seek to change and limit existing sites of power to foster and further inclusion and social justice (Stammers, 1999). Holston (1998) argues that the erosion of certain rights via-à-vis the state in the last half century have contributed to a search for new ways to realize rights through new social movements "outside of the normative and institutional definition of the state and its legal codes" (52). These movements aim to "transform the very political order in which they operate" (Alvarez, Dagnino, & Escobar, 1998: 8, quoted in Desmarais, 2007: 24–25) and are constituted by and constitutive of new ideas about democracy. They "give rise to subnational as well as transnational modes of citizenship" (Benhabib, 2004: 217). Such imaginaries about communities of people dedicated to agroecological change constitute a political imaginary that Wittman (2010) identifies as "agrarian citizenship." This conceptual frame places the allegiance of farmers and other stakeholders in the food system with nature and communities rather than with the state or corporations.

Wittman (2010) writes, "Agrarian communities with long-standing relationships and rights to the land have been disconnected from the ecological basis of citizenship by rural modernization strategies based on the separation of nature from culture" (91). By transferring the power of the sovereign from the state to nature, broadly defined, food sovereignty seeks to reconnect eaters of all kinds with the land that sustains life, in a reversal of the modernist separation of nature from culture (Latour, 1993). Wittman (2010) also argues that producers and consumers are separated from each other not only in the separation of rural and urban but also through trade and specialization strategies promoted by modern agriculture; the modern state, which forbids any trade not sanctioned by the state; and city planning, which excludes food production from the space of the city. The rights of communities to defend nature from corporations and the state are at the heart of self-governance ordinances.

Community Self-Governance Ordinances

The so-called food sovereignty ordinances that were passed in Maine in 2011 were written by activists inspired by the Community Environmental Legal Defense Fund. CELDF began in the 1990s as an organization dedicated to protecting communities in Pennsylvania from companies that were polluting water as well as from industrial natural-resource extraction and land-speculating developers. While working within the system by challenging permits, requesting environmental reviews, and so on, CELDF's strategies began to show success, but only in deferring the inevitable. Thomas Linzey, the group's founder, realized that until communities had the right to prevent companies from polluting or developing, all they could legally do was delay the process (Yeoman, 2013).

The self-governance ordinances evolved from work with communities that had failed to prevent polluting industries from operating, because they were not able to preempt the power of corporations. According to the CELDF website, "The communities being sued for their attempts to regulate or prohibit gas drilling and fracking are the ones that adopted *non*-rights-based ordinances. They base their ordinances on state regulatory law and receive the blessings of municipal solicitors that the ordinances are legal. And when the corporations sue, the laws are stacked on behalf of the corporations: violations of their constitutional and civil rights. The corporations win. The communities lose" (CELDF, 2015).

Linzey realized that while civil disobedience is an important tool of resistance, it has power only as an organizing tool, not a legal one (Yeoman, 2013). According to Linzey, asserting supremacy over state and federal government is, by definition, an illegal act. He realized that the answer, then, was not just to disobey in order to call attention to injustice and to organize around community rights but to do the additional work within the legal system required to expand rights to people, communities, and nature and to simultaneously impose limits on the rights of corporations. This realization led him to develop a four-pronged approach to self-government that identifies the source of disempowerment and spaces of resistance within the legal structures of the state.

According to Gail Darrell of CELDF, communities must work within what is called the "box of allowable action or activism." This box is created by four different functions of governance that limit community action. The first is the power of the state to preempt local governance, elaborated on above as Dillon's Rule. The second is the rights of corporations to be treated as individuals and to circumvent commerce laws. The third is that, legally, human work and the environment are treated as property, or commodities that can be exchanged and claimed through money. A laborer has the right to sell his or her labor in a market, just as a property owner (and sometimes the state) can buy and sell land and natural resources through a permitting and regulatory process. The last is the regulatory process, which bears some explanation.

CELDF identifies the regulatory process as the "Regulatory Fallacy," which sees the state as an agent that "permits" or facilitates economic activity, rather than defining limits to it. Darrell explains,

> We call it a fallacy because the regulatory structure is treated as though it prevents harm when actually it does the opposite. It legalizes the harm. So you think . . . I can go to hearings and I can talk about the damage that's going to come in my community and then the agency will not permit the project because they understand it will hurt my town. . . . The Department of Environmental Services functions to facilitate permitting business and industry. . . . So you think you're going to go to the hearing and you think you are going to get it resolved and actually nothing you say in the hearing must be considered before the permit issues. The

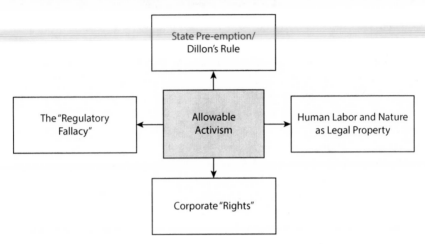

FIGURE 8. Box of allowable activism for communities. (Darrell, personal communication, 2013)

law is very careful [about this]. [Your testimony] *may be* considered. It doesn't say it *must be* considered. So we can go to the hearing, 60 people can testify and the permit will issue anyway, because the agency's function is to facilitate that process. And if the applicant fills out everything correctly, the permit must issue. It's the corporations' rights that are superior to the community's welfare. That's what the system was built to do.

According to Darrell, self-governance ordinances thus work against all of these legal constraints. They have a community bill of rights, including a statement asserting local self-governance, a set of prohibitions of certain activities (i.e., fracking), and a clause stripping corporations of their federally protected rights. The community bill of rights includes the right to clean air, the right to water, the right to soil, the right to self-government, and the rights of nature. Darrell says, "The rights of nature elevate nature to a place where we can actually speak of it as a person and protect it as a person, like your daughter, who can't speak for herself, so we have to advocate for her. It's actually lifting the ecosystem out of property status where it's currently in, so that it can be protected." The ordinances also have a key piece stating that the local community will acquiesce to state government only when higher-scale laws accord with the municipality's laws. Darrell again explains, "When state law protects the people in the community and also preserves that community, and doesn't violate the rights claimed in the rights in the ordinance, we'll obey state law and we'll obey all the federal laws. But when state and federal pre-emption comes in and tries to tell you that you must have GE food in your supermarket and your farmers markets and on your fields, we disagree. We say that's a violation of the community's rights and so this ordinance overrides the whole state and federal preemption when it's used that way."

A key feature of the ordinances protecting communities from natural resource extraction or industrial development projects includes stripping corporations of free speech, equal protection, and due process rights. The ordinances also take aim at protections offered to corporations by commerce and contract laws that "puts rights of property and commerce over people, nature and communities" (Linzey, quoted in Yeoman, 2013: 12). In short, the ordinances deny the rights associated with "corporate personhood" and assert a right to self-governance that subverts federal supremacy laws that protect corporations.

HANCOCK COUNTY ORDINANCES

The Hancock County (Maine) Ordinances were drafted and passed in order to protect small-scale farmers from what they perceived as threats to their operations in the form of food safety laws. According to Heather Retberg, a farmer and representative of Food for Maine's Future, these threats are issued by the FDA and USDA to protect the interests of corporations: "Right now 'Big Food' corporations use the regulatory agencies as a vehicle for their own interests. . . . These big food industries are now heavily represented in the rulemaking bodies of the USDA and FDA. They are the ones writing the rules—under the guise of food safety. Food safety rules could more accurately be called Big Food Protection Acts."

Retberg argues that state and federal regulations are out of touch with the needs of local communities, farmers, and consumers. The ordinances reflect fears held and articulated by many that state regulatory apparatuses exist to promote corporate interests at the expense of small-scale producers and consumers. Retberg, like many food sovereignty advocates, says that decision making is more effective at the local level than at higher levels and that the scaling up of power and control in the food system intentionally denies fundamental rights to citizens.

> Unfortunately, the FDA and USDA are extending their authority to oversee local farm food production. The USDA has put a legal mechanism into place that says anytime the Quality Assurance and Regulation Division [QAR] of our Maine Department of Agriculture makes rules, those rules must be "equal to" or greater than the USDA rules. So, if you go to Augusta to weigh in on the rules and tell the QAR that you trust your farmer or the neighbor who bakes bread and don't need the QAR to be an intermediary for you, it won't matter. The structure is in place already that denies your participation in the decision-making process that governs your food.

According to Retberg, the Local Food and Community Self-Governance Ordinances enacted in several of Maine's townships in Hancock County aim to address three questions raised by the scaling up of power over agricultural activities from the subnational state to the federal level in ways that are detrimental to small-scale producers and consumers: "Who decides what happens in our communities right now? What kind of relationship do we want to have with each other? What rights do we want to encode into law?" Answering these questions with food sovereignty ordinances makes good on the claim Retberg articulates, that "we have the right within our own community to determine what that community will look like and what relationships we have with each other. Town meetings are our most direct form of participatory democracy. Local control is essential to the growth of our local food system."

Six home rule townships in Maine passed the so-called food sovereignty ordinances in April 2011 during the spring town meeting cycle. The ordinances were intended to protect town residents engaged in direct sale of farm goods from the inspection and licensure requirements that were designed for larger-scale processing and long-distance agricultural trade. The ordinances exempt all food prepared for community events, such as church suppers or fundraisers, from federal or state licensure or inspection. They also exempt processed or unprocessed food sold in a direct exchange between a farmer and a consumer for his or her home consumption from state licensure or inspection. Representative Craig Hickman, in support of these efforts, also sponsored several "food sovereignty" bills—which ultimately failed—in the state assembly. They were meant to provide state-level protection to farmers who engage in poultry processing, sales of raw milk, and direct sales of farm stuffs. Dan Brown erroneously believed that his right to sell raw milk was protected, not only by the municipal ordinances but also by the state's home rule doctrine, which protects the rights of municipalities to govern. The degree to which that was true for Hancock County townships was tested and established by Brown's case.

DAN BROWN AND HOME RULE

When Dan Brown had his day in court, the judge ruled that Brown was (1) selling raw milk without being in possession of a milk distributor's license, (2) selling raw milk without having the necessary "warning" label, and (3) selling other foods prepared in his home kitchen without being in possession of a retail food license. His defense stated that these activities were permitted under home rule and the ordinances. The court declined to permit him shelter under home rule, saying that (1) milk was not expressly included as a local food, (2) an exemption for local food already existed in Maine state law, but it did not include milk, and (3) home rule protects actions that "do not frustrate state law" (*State of Maine v. Brown*, 2014). The state of Maine's concern over Dan Brown is not that he is selling raw milk but that he is doing it outside the regulatory framework that legitimizes the state's authority to determine the safety of the food product. In other words, only the state, rather than the producer or the consumer or the community, has the power to deem whether food is safe to consume or not, regardless of whether people are willing to take the risk. A self-governance ordinance, according to the judge, "frustrates" the state's power to regulate.

Almy (2013) suggests that regulatory authority in the state of Maine is not just about the power to decide safety; it also provides the power to "define the state's view as to what constitutes an ideal food system" (801). State statutes identify agriculture as "a major industry" and underscore its importance to the "state's overall economy" (Maine Legislative Statutes, 2014). They also stress the significance of "family farming" and agricultural ways of life, which regulation is meant to protect. Almy points out that regulatory mechanisms at the state level exist to facilitate the preservation of agricultural livelihoods, not just to ensure food safety. According to Almy, the failure to distinguish between farming as a livelihood and farming as an industry requires that small-scale farmers have no choice but to opt out of the system. In addition, the failure to distinguish between industry and livelihoods makes the state regulatory apparatus a vehicle for facilitating the industrialization of the food system, in much the way that Darrell of CELDF says the "regulatory fallacy" works to permit environmentally destructive practices.

Almy (2013) argues that the state was correct in its ruling in the Brown case, but had it seen the role of legislation and agriculture, as well as the health and safety of both producers and consumers, in a different light, it very well could have found the ordinances appropriate instances of home rule. He writes, "The question in *Brown* then, is not whether the existing regulatory scheme is fully consistent with and facilitates the intended purposes of agriculture, but whether the *ordinance* achieves these goals" (803, original emphasis). The court saw the ordinances as "frustrating" the ability of the state to regulate and thus, in the state's view, failing to achieve the aims of agriculture as the state saw it. In the ruling in *State of Maine v. Brown* (2014), the justice writes, "It is axiomatic that a municipality may only add to the requirements of the statute, it may not take away from those requirements unless *permitted* to do so otherwise" (9). Municipalities must be permitted to view agriculture as a livelihood; in this case, they were expressly forbidden from doing so.

LIMITING CORPORATE RIGHTS

In a speech to Pennsylvania Women's Agricultural Network in 2012, Heather Retberg put the local food and self-governance ordinances in the context of a broader struggle for the rights of people to self-govern, rights that she says are not realized yet: "Now is the time that gravitational pull must bring that pendulum back down towards people over profit, natural persons over corporate persons and local communities over political parties. Corporations are the legal 'children' of the state, but the state derives its authority from the people. If we the people are to maintain this authority, we are going to need to work in that direction and assert the 'natural authority' [that] Jefferson penned in the Declaration [and which] nowhere appears in our constitution."

Gail Darrell echoes this statement and links the struggle for self-governance and protection from corporate control of the economy to the civil and women's rights movements. "The law needs to change. That's how we got the Civil Rights Act in place—the students sat at the lunch counters. They didn't think they were going to get lunch. They knew they were going to get arrested. But they knew that if they broke the law, they would bring it to the attention of the law and get it changed. The same was true with women. They voted when it was illegal to prove that the law was unjust, and that law was changed."

Like Retberg, Darrell asserts that this is a longer and broader struggle, adding that food sovereignty is requesting "rights that are not yet enumerated." She elaborated on an example of a friend who said the work on the ordinances is illegal: "My answer is it isn't illegal, it's just not legal yet. Law is constantly changed to adapt to society." Darrell's faith in the process of enumerating rights and enacting new legislation is precisely what Cadman (2010) argues rights are and what governance does. Citizens and governments engage in a participatory practice, and rights are used as a place from which to advocate for changes to the juridical structures governing social, political, and economic life. The idea that rights to self-governance don't exist yet does not mean they never will. To obtain them, however, means that those rights must include a limit on the rights of corporations. Darrell explains, "The way the law is set up, the contracts between corporations and the state when they get their charter means they are on an equal level. Our municipalities are not. We are subordinate. We are creatures of the state and as such people are not citizens of their towns. They have citizenship with the state and country, but not their towns."

Darrell argues that overturning or outlawing corporate personhood laws are key to success, not only for self-governance in a general sense, but also for food sovereignty law or local food and self-governance ordinances in particular. She says of the Hancock County ordinances and their advocates,

> The corporate piece must be there because that's the fight they are picking, they just don't see it that way. They think it's state regulatory issues, but its way bigger than that and they just don't see it. The state pre-emptive piece needs to be in there even though they are a home rule state. . . . Even in home rule communities that what the state permits as a municipality, they cannot ban. When you claim rights you need to put them in the bill of rights section and then make a prohibition that would stop anything that would violate the rights. There has to be that balance in the law. Otherwise the courts could argue that the law doesn't address that issue

explicitly. It can't do anything but prevent corporations from coming into your meetings and [having] a place to speak or vote.

In theory, Maine's home rule structure should grant municipalities rights to determine legislation, but the "supremacy clause" is prioritized and interpreted by courts to restrict the actions of municipalities (Bower, 1985: 314). Thus collective rights based in the territorial spaces of the action are key to the protections that the Blue Hill communities seek, both in terms of rights to be protected from corporations and in terms of collective rights to govern exchange. Federal law does not recognize a generalized individual right to consume foods of one's choosing, and thus individual rights cannot protect or extend the rights that food sovereignty seeks. The radical change food sovereignty envisions requires both subsidiarity—decision making at a local level—and the collective right to self-governance.

Retberg articulates self-governance as a prerequisite for justice and rights in her public speeches: "An agency of our representative government can't take from us, by re-defining who we are and what we do—our right to alter, re-form or totally change government when our safety and happiness require it. . . . When we asserted our right to self-governance of our food system in our towns in Maine, we are fundamentally, foundationally, going back to our roots. We reject the right of governmental agencies to define us or what we do in a way that undermines our safety and happiness" (Retberg, 2012).

This assertion of local autonomy over the productive resource of the food system is a new and critically important assertion of space and territory, which has important implications for the way citizenship is constructed. Because food sovereignty discourse so often identifies the problems of the food system as lying with the state, it is reasonable to ask what role the state might have in changing itself. Examinations of food sovereignty practice, however, reveal a strategy of reterritorialization of space that claims allegiance to the moral universals of ecological and community health. This strategy has more to do with resisting neoliberalism and recasting the relationship between citizens and the state than waiting for the state to change in response to demands from its citizens.

Dan Brown and his supporters learned the hard way that ordinances, even those protected by home rule, must not "frustrate" the intent of federal law. When federal law supports the interests of interstate trade or the accumulation of transnational capital over individual or collective rights to health or food, the (neo)liberal state becomes visible. In this case, such visibility occurred through the vehicle of food safety legislation. Almy (2013) argues that "safety regulations that arguably limit the consumers ability to obtain food products of their choice

are seen by some as tantamount to restrictions upon the exercise of a fundamental right" (794). While an ordinance such as those passed in Maine "rejects
as unlawful any state or federal interference with the rights asserted" (Almy,
2013: 795), these rights happen to be ones that the state chooses not to protect,
largely due to its fundamental rights to regulate trade through the Commerce
Clause (Kurtz, Trauger, & Passidomo, 2013). Ordinances can, however, establish the right of self-governance if they target carefully, in this case, focusing on
corporations and putting limits on their rights. Ordinances also have the radical
potential to protect and expand rights for groups, rather than individuals, when
they overtly emphasize the collective rights of a community.

The growth in multiple, overlapping, and increasingly global affiliations coincides with the crisis in Westphalian state sovereignty and the subsequent splin-
tering of political affiliations (Benhabib, 2004). Since the 1980s national states
have engaged in a variety of transnational and supranational political economic
arrangements, such as the European Union. This relative decline in state sovereignty coincides with an increase in the devolution of state power to subnational
state political units, such as municipalities and nongovernmental, community-
based organizations. In the United States, the development of the "local state"
(Storey, 2001: 124) includes such problematic programs as 287(g) (also known
as "Secure Communities"), which deputizes local police to arrest and detain
individuals suspected of immigration violations (Coleman, 2009). The devolution of state power can also take the form of communities seeking solutions
to problems within localities, such as the development of city-scale policies on
climate change (Rice, 2010) or the extension of municipal-scale voting rights
to noncitizens (Varsanyi, 2005). These shifts in the scale of governance to the
alternative spaces that food sovereignty calls for constitute a reterritorializing of
power, potentially changing the meaning and nature of citizenship and rights.

Holston (1998) asserts that given the erosion of certain kinds of rights, citizens should seek alternative sources of belonging and entities different from
the state to which to claim allegiance. Engagement with these movements, primarily via social networking technologies and membership in organizations,
establishes multiple allegiances with affiliations at (multiple) spatial scales below
and beyond the reach of the state—local, regional, and transnational scales.
Holston argues that the dominance of citizenship at the scale of the state is
simply a spatial strategy of modernist development, which aims to create a kind
of citizenship that is generative of itself over time and space and thus normalizes an allegiance to the national state. Insurgent citizenship asserts new sorts
of legitimate allegiances and affiliations that generate different, mutable, and
perhaps "overlapping" or "variegated" visions of political space and belonging.

Liberal sovereignty can be read as neoliberal governance, which places responsibility for one's health on the individual, but only within the sphere of
options the state has deemed healthful or right. In the case of raw milk or pas-

tured poultry, the only legal option available to eaters is the one that facilitates the accumulation of corporate capital. Challenges to state sovereignty and hegemony question taken-for-granted assumptions about the mutual exclusivity and territorial fixity of sovereign state power and open new conversations about how to define citizenship, democracy, and rights as well as about the role of social movements in defining, securing, and fulfilling those rights and responsibilities. The Maine self-governance ordinances can potentially be read as libertarian responses to the state, but when read back through CELDF's revisions that include an emphasis on collective rights to govern and limits to corporate power, perhaps they reveal an entirely radical new vision of democracy instead.

PART III

CHAPTER FIVE

Re/territorializing Food Security

Manoomin *Gift Economies*

The rice gives, so we give.

Anishinabek elder

In response to the Rome Summit on Food Security in 1996, NGOs articulated in point 6 of their declaration that "food cannot be considered as a commodity because of its social and cultural dimension." Following from this, and as a result of much debate and discussion, the Nyéléni declarations state that part of the struggle for food sovereignty includes fighting against the *"privatisation and commodification* of food, basic and public services, knowledge, land, water, seeds, livestock and our natural heritage" (Nyéléni, 2007: 10, emphasis added). Food sovereignty narratives make clear that treating food as a commodity and commodifying the things that make food production possible (i.e., land, inputs) do not and cannot contribute to true and lasting food security. Less clear is what this means for food supply systems, globally and locally.

This chapter attempts to shed some light on existing alternative food systems that practice antiprivatization and anticommodification. By tracing the historical process of the commodification of food through the social and geographical construction of commodities and consumers, I hope to demonstrate that commodification is a socially constructed process and thus it is possible to resist it. Throughout the twenty-first century, independent producers in the United States and elsewhere were turned into consumers through the promotion of narratives of modernity and technological advancement among farming families (Neth, 1995; Jellison, 1993). Van der Ploeg (2010) refers to this as "state induced modernization" (2) which was forced on farmers in the name of food safety and for the interests of capital. The exchange of food products such as raw milk that do not pass through the industrial food supply chain is thus sanctioned and criminalized (Paxson, 2008).

In this context, then, how does food sovereignty hope to disentangle food from the commodity system that claims to produce both safe and cheap food?

I argue that one way to escape the commodification of food is to never make it a commodity in the first place. As elaborated on elsewhere in this book, permaculture practices, use of public space, and alternative labor arrangements all contribute to producing food that does not become a commodity. Non/post/anti-capitalist exchange is the next step in continuing this effort. I use the exchange of *manoomin* (wild rice) in the Anishinabek communities on the White Earth Reservation in Minnesota to elaborate on how this might be achieved. The exchange of wild rice through reciprocal social economies persists on White Earth in spite of the way the corporate food regime seeks to monetize all exchanges. The persistence of noncapitalist exchange in the face of widespread pressure to commodify food is significant and bears further scrutiny for its relevance to food sovereignty.

The White Earth Land Recovery project (WELRP) is an organization that operates under the banner of food sovereignty, and many of its projects are geared toward reclaiming land, language, traditional diets, and local economies. While my interest in WELRP initially brought me to White Earth, this chapter is not about this organization; rather, it is about the refusals of people living at White Earth to make food a commodity and their maintenance of nonmonetary exchanges of food. Guthman (2008b) and others (Alkon & Mares, 2012) make it quite clear that we can't buy and sell our way out of the multiple problems that industrial agriculture has presented to the modern food system. Some would argue that we need more "nested" markets (van der Ploeg, 2010) or "embedded" markets (Hinrichs, 2000) so that farmers can continue to have livelihoods, but food sovereignty seems to suggest some other radical alternative in many of its declarations. What if we don't commodify food at all?

Indigenous Rights and Food Security

The Nyéléni Declaration specifically identifies protecting the rights of indigenous populations to hunt, fish, and rice as key elements of achieving food security. Under the heading "What We Are Fighting For" several bullet points list the conditions that are required to bring about food security for the world's population, especially for the most vulnerable. The list includes recognition of women's rights, fair wages for workers, respect for traditional knowledge, and rehabilitation of rural environments. According to this framework, genuine and effective agrarian reform *"defends and recovers the territories of indigenous peoples [and] ensures fishing communities' access and control over their fishing areas and eco-systems"* (Nyéléni, 2007: 9, emphasis added). While the rights to hunt and fish are important and will be briefly discussed in this chapter, I focus on rights to gather and manage wild rice in the lakes and streams of northern Minnesota.

WHITE EARTH RESERVATION

White Earth Reservation was created on March 19, 1867, during a meeting of Chippewa chiefs and President Andrew Johnson. At thirty-six by thirty-six miles square, the reservation covers 837,000 acres in northwestern Minnesota in the counties of Becker, Clearwater, and Mahnomen. It is home to over twenty-five thousand White Earth Anishinabek and includes 3,343 total households, 1,060 of which are headed by an American Indian.[1] One of seven Anishinabek reservations in northern Minnesota, White Earth is faced with many food security and health-related challenges. According to Indian Health Services on the White Earth Reservation, approximately 30 percent of the population has diabetes, and an increasing number of children are developing Type 2 diabetes. The reservation is classified as a rural food desert because it has no grocery stores and residents must travel long distances by car to buy food (USDA, 2009; MPR, 2011). In this respect, White Earth is not alone: nearly 60 percent of counties with an American Indian majority population suffer from severe food insecurity (Feeding America, 2011). The state of Minnesota classifies White Earth as the poorest reservation in Minnesota; over half of White Earth residents have incomes below the poverty level, and the unemployment rate is 25 percent.

Many residents of White Earth live in tribal housing projects, as a result of being forced off the land through allotment and illegal annexation. Privatization of commonly held land and resources was facilitated through a system of allotment. Natives and non-Natives alike see the reservation as a kind of "final solution" (Aaron, personal communication, 2013) in which rebellion against settler colonialism was shut down. The land set aside for the White Earth Reservation is rich in timber and agricultural and water resources, and it was thought that allotment would enroll the Anishinabek into the emerging market economy in Minnesota (Meyer, 1994). Under the Dawes Act of 1887, communal landholdings were divided into 160-acre plots to be distributed to each enrolled member of the eligible tribe who elected to live at White Earth. The logic behind this was supported by a white supremacist "faith in the almost magical ability of private property to transform Indians' collective values" (Meyer, 1994: 1). The remaining land was declared "surplus" and the Nelson Act of 1889 enabled non-Natives to purchase it. This resulted in more than 90 percent of the original reservation land ending up in the hands of various off-reservation entities, such as a Boy Scout camp and the federal government. There was considerable resistance to allotment among the Indians, due to tribal notions of property and the economy as well as intertribal conflict related to the belief of some that allotment represented a zero-sum game for tribal members (Meyer, 1994).

Winona LaDuke, an Anishinabek leader who ran as a vice presidential candidate for the Green Party in 1996 and 2000, started the White Earth Land Recovery Project in 1989 to advocate for the return of lands to the White Earth

Tribe. LaDuke's grandmother was tricked into ceding her land allotment when she signed a piece of paper in exchange for food supplies in the middle of a harsh Minnesota winter (LaDuke, personal communication, 2010). Tribal notions of land never included enclosure or privatization; as such, the idea of the sale of land was an ontological impossibility to LaDuke's grandmother and to most Native people at the time.

WELRP works on community organizing, education, cultural exchange, and civic engagement and aims to secure land, sacred items, language, and ceremonies, as well as to restore and strengthen traditional practices related to food and the economy. The harvest and sale of wild rice, a native grain, helps sustain the organization's activities, which also include a farm-to-school program in three elementary schools.

"Land sovereignty" is a key piece of food sovereignty demands and aims, for land is the key means of food production. In the United States, 96 percent of all farmland is owned by whites (Gilbert, Wood, & Sharp, 2002), a situation made possible by the systematic theft of productive land through the dispossession and marginalization of nonwhites. The return of land to the collective management of the White Earth Tribe will mean returning access to lakes and rivers where wild rice grows but where access is restricted via privatization: by tourists who own second homes on the lakes, by federal protection of national forests, and by prohibition by other nontribal entities. The lakes from which rice is harvested by hand are not owned by anyone in any real sense, not even the tribe, and therefore the value of the rice itself is determined more through use than exchange. Rice from the White Earth Reservation takes a variety of paths following harvest and processing. Some is sold to WELRP, which distributes it locally and nationally through the Native Harvest website. Some rice is sold to the tribe for redistribution on the reservation. The remainder is consumed in nearly every household and shared through cooperatives and through ritualized gifting.

FOOD SECURITY, TREATY RIGHTS, AND *MANOOMIN*

Wild rice (*Zizania palustris*) is a grain endemic to the lakes and ponds of the Upper Midwest and has provided a staple food for Anishinabek and other tribes living there for centuries. It is a species of aquatic grass not related to modern cultivated white rice (*Oryza sativa*). *Manoomin*, as it is called by the Anishinabek, has not been bred for commercial production until recently, and the rice in northern lakes and water bodies has evolved over time to be specific to watersheds, producing at least two distinct subspecies. Wild rice is propagated from seed that requires a muddy substrate commonly found in lakes and slow-moving streams in the Upper Midwest. It is sensitive to environmental disturbances, including and especially pollutants.[2] As a wild perennial, *manoomin* does not require cultivation, but native ricers often deliberately drop grain into

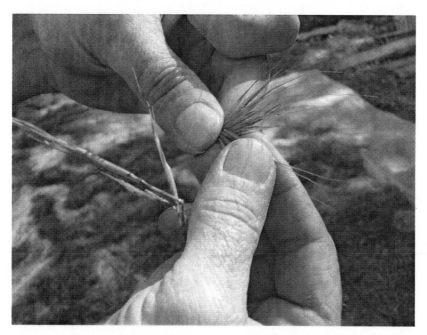

FIGURE 9. Freshly harvested wild rice before parching. (Author's photo)

the water as they harvest in a spiritual-ecological practice referred to as "seed-ing" to ensure the next year's harvest. Hybrid cultivars of wild rice have been grown in paddy cultivation with mechanical harvesting since the 1960s (Ven-num, 1988). California is the largest producer of cultivated "wild" rice today, with Native populations losing market share because of the high cost of produc-tion of *manoomin*. Wild rice is a high-fiber, high-protein, low-glycemic whole grain that is especially recommended for consumption by diabetics. The rights to gather subsistence food and the traditions that are associated with them have been radically altered through the disruptions that colonialism, genocide, and racism have visited on the Anishinabek.

In 1837 the Chippewa/Ojibwe tribes of the Upper Midwest, under duress, ceded three million acres of territory to the United States, while retaining some hunting, fishing, and ricing rights. These rights have not been honored by either federal or state governments, and Anishinabek tribal members currently engage in a variety of political battles to regain or retain rights that are increasingly undermined by the commercial ricing, sport fishing, and hunting industries in Minnesota. The most notable court case involving ricing rights in Minnesota, in 1980, involved two defendants, Everett Keezer and James Kier, who were charged with ricing off the reservation without a license. Keezer and Kier con-tested the charges, arguing that their rights to rice without a license were codified in numerous treaties. The state of Minnesota argued that rights to hunt, fish, and gather were nullified in later treaties, and furthermore, the relinquishing of territory included the relinquishing of usufruct rights. The state's interest in preventing the use of its territory for hunting, fishing, and gathering by Natives reflects its keen desire to protect the profitable tourism industry, which rests on many of the resources used for subsistence means by the Anishinabek (Indian Fishing and Hunting Rights, 2014).

According to the dissenting opinion in *State v. Keezer*, the judges who ruled against the Anishinabek defendants were biased by "culturally-bound conceptions of property rights" (J. Whal, dissenting, quoted in Hawley, 1980: 373). To identify the bias of the judges as rooted in cultural differences misses the larger point that denying access to hunting and fishing off-reservation is a denial of historical rights as well as an effective tool of genocide. That the state of Minnesota supports tourism over the rights of its indigenous populations also reveals the degree to which political decision making promotes capital over the welfare of people. The denial of treaty rights is as effective as all the other forms of assimilation that were used to destroy the integrity of Native communities in the past (Meyer, 1994). The decision is also consistent with a long history of forcing Natives out of subsistence economies and into a capitalist economy of food. Reluctance to relate to food as a commodity and resistance to treating it as such are not new, but they are increasingly seen as revolutionary stances.

Commodities and Their Afterlives

The Nyéléni delegates are clear that the commodification of food is antithetical to food security and is ultimately the source of hunger. In their view, when food is a commodity, people become hungry when they are too poor to buy it. The modernist approach to food security has been to produce more food and make it cheaper, but no matter how cheap or plentiful food is, if consumers have no income they will remain hungry. Producers are also marginalized by this approach, because the cheaper food becomes, the poorer farmers become, as prices fall and the limits of overproduction are reached (Goodman & Redclift, 1991). Subsidizing food or granting various forms of assistance are one part of the solution to hunger, but food aid to the needy is increasingly contested and politically unpopular (Robinson, 2004). Several alternative food justice projects have worked to stop making food a commodity through urban gardening (Gottlieb & Joshi, 2010), but these are also politically contested spaces of production. In what follows, I discuss how and why food became a commodity and suggest what is needed to establish a system in which food does not become a commodity.

COMMODITIES AND COMMODITIZATION

Commodities acquire their value, according to Marx (1867/1977) through their transfer to someone else, for whom the commodity may have what he called a "use-value." The conditions established in the transaction determine the "exchange value" of the product, which is thought to be separate from its use value. Commodities, according to Marx, are distinguished from other products of labor because they begin life as an object that is intended to be exchanged. Thus food or any other thing becomes a commodity when it passes through a particular, usually monetary, exchange. However, Appadurai (1988) asserts that commodification is just "one phase in the life of some things" (17) and defines a commodity as a thing in a "situation in which its exchangeability (past, present or future) for some other thing is its socially relevant feature" (13). Identifying products as characterized by their "situation" and their social relevance signals that commodities are socially and culturally constructed and, as such, have multiple lives. In this formulation, anything has the potential to become a commodity.

Identifying things as commodities through their appearance in certain "situations" moves the focus from the thing itself to the social context through which a thing travels. The problems that commoditization poses for food security, then, are not inherent in the commodities themselves but lie in the process, arguably a capitalist one, that produces them and through which they are distributed. The "socially relevant feature" of food as a commodity is its value in exchange, rather than its ability to provide sustenance and nutrition through its use. In the context of food production, Harriss (1982) argues that the "process of commoditization is the linking of rural household producers with capitalist production" (22). Friedmann (1980), focusing also on the household and social reproduction, remarks that commoditization is the "process of deepening commodity relations within the cycle of reproduction" (6). In other words, commoditization turns both the productive and reproductive functions of the rural household from meeting subsistence needs toward the act of consumption, such as purchasing inputs for the farm. Jellison (1993) identifies this process as coincident with the cultivation of middle-class ideologies in rural communities as agriculture modernized in the United States during the mid-twentieth century.

Van der Ploeg (2010) argues that states and capitalism working in the interests of agribusiness—a combined force he calls the "food Empire"—force farmers to modernize or be left behind. This forced shift toward consuming more has the effect of producing food that has only one socially relevant feature: its exchange value. Resistance to the commoditization process is enacted through "self-provisioning" or, in the terminology of transaction cost theory (Williamson, 1981), "making" instead of "buying." Self-provisioning, according to van der

Ploeg (2010), is not mere subsistence but a process that reduces dependence on external resources and allows for the accumulation of ecological capital to the resource base. Van der Ploeg's (2010) framework is useful in that it identifies particular interventions in the "commodity situation" of contemporary agriculture that change the balance of commodity and noncommodity relations on farms. He argues that this is important because the more a farm is distanced from dependence on external inputs, the more autonomy and relative power it has to construct alternatives.

Developing alternatives, however, also requires the reconfiguration of the social relationships that shape food exchanges, or the "situation" through which food and other things travel. One approach to changing the social context of food is through decommodifying it. Decommodification is a moment or situation in which a thing destined to be exchanged for money is diverted from its path so that its exchange value is eliminated or changed. Food banks are often thought to be spaces of decommodification in which food becomes an entitlement, with its most socially relevant feature being that of alleviating short-term food insecurity. Henderson (2004) argues that decommodification also produces value elsewhere in the supply chain and as such is not a total transformation of the value (exchange or use) of the product. Decommodification is thus about creating a new social context for the production of food security through food items that still have use and exchange values. Henderson's work demonstrates that the significance of decommodification lays not so much with taking a food item out of circuits of exchange value but in the creation of alternative social contexts that allow for different value sets, such as self-sufficiency or limiting the commercialization of food (Boulanger, 2010).

Gibson-Graham (2006) suggest that this process is part of the development of a postcapitalist economy, which they argue is premised on the production of new economic subjectivities. The primary mode of relating in postcapitalist ways is through generating networks of interdependence (Trauger & Passidomo, 2012). By way of example, Burke (2012) found that in a postconflict community in Medellin, Colombia, the construction of an alternative economy was central to building local capacities, collective welfare, and a system of interdependent cooperation. The barter systems and alternative currencies he investigated were designed and facilitated through alliances between the middle and working class, peasants, and others. Burke found that the opportunity to control more of the process of production and consumption gave the participants a significant sense of autonomy. The lack, however, of a sustained effort in changing economic subjectivities resulted in an overt focus on anticapitalism that did little to change the underlying capitalist structure within which they worked. As Burke's work demonstrates, a stridently anticapitalist approach, often utilized by advocates of decommodification as well as food sovereignty, also does little to change the social context within which poverty and hunger are (re)produced.

GIFT ECONOMIES

A gift economy is one social context through which goods pass. It is a form of a reciprocal social economy, in which food or other goods and services are exchanged through ritualized giving, usually at important social events or as a form of respect in more mundane settings (Curry, 2003). A key component of a gift economy is that goods are given without explicit understanding that a similar good will be given in exchange at some later date (Malinowski, 1922). Reciprocation often happens, but the original gift is generally not assumed to be given as one part of a transaction. The analysis of gift economies and how they work originates in anthropological work on "premodern" or nonmarket economies. As such, many of the conclusions drawn about gift economies reflect anthropological attitudes about the rules and customs of premodern societies, most notably that they are ahistorical, backward, and distinct from commodity economies. There is also much debate in anthropological circles (and there is not time or space enough to rehearse it here) about whether a gift economy, because of its complex social context, even constitutes an economy at all. To focus on this debate, however, elides the more important features of the functions of a gift economy (Gregory, 1982); the function of the gift is less about the circulation of things than about the cooperative survival of groups (Mauss, 1954).

While it is widely thought that the commodity situation dominates most transactions, the transformation from premodern to modern economies is incomplete. According to White and Williams (2012), the world "should be more properly understood as a largely non-capitalist landscape composed of economic plurality, wherein relations are often embedded in non-commodified practices such as mutual aid, reciprocity, co-operation and inclusion" (1636). Precapitalist modes of exchange abound, even as they are marked as backward or primitive by a state-market nexus concerned with the production and appropriation of surplus. Offer (1997) calls these exchanges "relations of regard" in which things are transferred between people as "gifts," as part of an interpersonal process of communication. According to Offer, the gift economy has a number of features, including "voluntary transfer; an expectation of reciprocity; and [motivation] by a desire for regard, over and above any gains from trade." Furthermore, the gift is "unpriced, often unpriceable; and gift establishes [a] repetitive, self-enforcing bond, which facilitates trade" (457).

Appadurai (1988), however, asserts that gift economies operate within the system of commodity exchange, because "gifts" retain their exchange value and remain in a social context in which exchange is still a "socially relevant feature" (83). Appadurai (2006) thus troubles the distinction between commodity and gift, suggesting that gifts in any economy move from commodity forms to gift forms and back as part of their circulation through any given *sphere of exchange*. The essential feature of any economy—commodity or otherwise—is the way "transactions that surround things are invested with the properties of social relations" (Appadurai, 2006: 15). In other words, the meaning attached to the exchange shapes the larger social relations within the economy. In tribal, indigenous, or preindustrial societies, the gift is an important medium of exchange, as perhaps the overly well-documented "potlatch" custom of Pacific Northwest First Nations demonstrates. Gifting has a variety of meanings and functions, including some of the insurance, financial, and welfare systems now provided by the liberal state and market in capitalist economies. Gift economies also function as a mechanism for civil society to mitigate the failure of the state or markets to provide for people.

According to Appadurai (2006), gift economies reflect and reify particular kinds of social relationships that shape exchanges of property. Gifting approximates a kind of transfer of property rights from one person to another, and the way property is viewed underpins the entire system. Anarchist political theory suggests that gift economies resolve the contradictions of capitalism, particularly those that consolidate capital in the hands of a few, producing poverty. Kropotkin (1907) premised his vision of a world without currency on mutualist exchanges of property made through voluntary cooperative participation. In this vision of the world, as long as there are enough goods and services to meet all needs, hunger could not exist as long as everyone participated in the system. In this system, no one could own things, and therefore it would not be possible to deny anyone access to them. In addition, the advantage of gift exchanges, in terms of political struggle against van Der Ploeg's food Empire, is that the gift is hard to track and regulate. Because it is often not monetized, its exchange is not taxable, and surplus occurs only in the form of "regard" (Offer, 1997). If the gift is not in the form of money, or is in the form of something that has never been commodified, capital also cannot be appropriated from its exchange (i.e., taxes or profit).

Within the context of a liberal state, the odds of developing and sustaining a noncommoditized food system, as envisioned by the NGOs that authored the 1996 concept of food sovereignty, seem slim. The Nyéléni delegates themselves may have understood this, or at least they tried to be clearer about how food sovereignty could work within the existing regulatory and exchange structures in a market economy. As such, they identify important roles for local market exchanges in the effort to achieve food security, as well as a central role for the state in regulating and controlling international-scale markets. But let's assume for the purposes of argument that food sovereignty aims to shift the balance of commoditization as far back toward production as it can be pushed. Making this argument opens up space to consider what social contexts and what spheres of exchange might (or must?) exist to facilitate the production of food as an anticommodity. In what follows, in addition to addressing the interpersonal relations around exchange, I also query how land, which is also a commodity, figures into these contexts and spheres.

Anticapitalist Exchange and the Commons

The concept of food as something that can be socially constructed as having an exchange value is part of the problem with so-called alternative food systems, including organic and Fair Trade (Alkon & Mares, 2012). As long as food is bought and sold, it will be subject to the disciplinary power of capitalism (Guthman, 1998). One avenue out of this paradox is that food should be produced in such a way that its most significant "socially relevant feature" is to provide sustenance, not profit. In what follows I address the production of alternative subjectivities that support such exchanges, followed by a discussion of the practices that I observed during several months of fieldwork on the White Earth Reservation in Minnesota. I conclude with a sobering discussion about the way these activities are criminalized, which both marginalizes a community that persists in noncommoditized exchanges and also enrolls more subjects in the commoditization process and continues processes of accumulation through dispossession.

ANTICAPITALIST SUBJECTIVITIES

Winona LaDuke, activist and writer, says, "Wild rice or *manoomin* is not just a food for the Anishinabek people; it is a way of life. *Manoomin* is the cornerstone of our ecosystem and our culture." According to the origin myths of the Anishinabek, they are supposed to live where the blueberries, strawberries, wild rice, and black bear all grow together. LaDuke says, "There is a migration story that a lot of cultural anthropologists like to start with, but our recorded histories go back beyond the time before the earth Turtle Island was even created. The sprits came here to prepare the place for us. We were star people then. The spirits made it for us and gave it to us to take care of. If we didn't, our people would be destroyed" (personal communication, 2010).

The preparations of the home for the Anishinabek included the making of a place with *manoomin*, or what is called "the food that grows on the water." In my conversations with other White Earth tribal members, the issue of cultural sovereignty continued to emerge as a dominant theme connected to food sovereignty. One White Earth woman said, "There can be no restoration of healthful diets and self-sufficiency without language, ritual and performance, and celebration of identity" (Betty).

As a clear demonstration of the linkages between healthful diets and cultural sovereignty, Anishinabek ceremonies that were criminalized as part of white settler colonialism include ritual sharing of wild rice, in addition to a variety of practices that reinforce and articulate the meaning of Anishinabek spirituality and identity. One such ceremony, featuring the tribal drum, is an important site of both the circulation of Native spiritual practices—sharing the pipe, speaking and singing in the Anishinabek language, honoring the drum and its history, installing new leaders in the community, and honoring women, warriors, and elders—as well as the circulation of food as a gift, both to the people and the spirits as an interconnected whole. As one visiting member of the Leech Lake Tribe said about the drum ceremony, "We keep the spirits alive and keep them with their people, who are feeding themselves so that the spirits are fed" (Jimmy).

A White Earth member talked about the drum ceremony in more practical terms: "The drum ceremony is critical for community health because it keeps people focused on tradition and traditional ways of life" (Don). This sentiment was echoed by Bob Shimek, who teaches kids about wild foods through WELRP. He says, "We are teaching them about the food, language, and culture. We need to stitch all those people together and give them something to hang on to." In this comment he is alluding to a narrative of destruction that must be countered by shoring up Anishinabek ways of life, knowledge, and values. In this sense, identity is constructed as part of an interlinked relation to food, nature, and place. This is evident in both origin stories like the one related above and in stories that foreshadow destruction and redemption.

A story about the destruction of the Anishinabek (and others) is one I heard frequently in my conversations with tribal members and leaders. The story begins with a grandfather speaking to the Anishinabek, telling of the importance of sharing *manoomin* with others, including the bullhead and the crane and the eagle and the black bear and so on. According to Bob Shimek, when the elder is finished with his story he adds one more thing: "The white man will make a big fire that will destroy all this, and some Anishinabek will be standing next to him". While Shimek's telling of the story focuses on modern environmental destruction in which all of us are complicit, another White Earth woman who related the same story to me suggested a different interpretation, one more focused on the interconnected cultural and environmental losses of modernization. "We are not losing the language. The language is losing us, because of the way we have become. Drug addiction, theft, loss of respect for elders. We were told that if we didn't take care of these gifts, they would be taken away from us. And we didn't take care of them. We have to return to the drum as part of our responsibility of overkilling animals in the forest through the fur trade" (Caroline).

She references the collapse of beaver and other fur-bearing animal populations in the Upper Midwest as a result of collusion between Anishinabek and French fur traders in the nineteenth century. Through the telling of this story, the elders teach lessons learned about management—both what happened and how to fix it. In this view, buying and selling life is antithetical to both Anishinabek recovery as a culture and their survival in the future.

Exchange

Embedded in the story about caring for the natural resources that support the Anishinabek way of life is a narrative about community food security in the form of sharing rice with others. In the past, the autumnal ricing season would supply each family with enough *manoomin* for one year and a bit extra for trading. Anything left would be distributed among the families, particularly to those without able-bodied adults and to the elderly. This practice, now dramatically changed, lives on in the ritual gifting of rice in many social interactions. For example, wild rice is given to the host, particularly elders, whenever a person is invited to a home. It is also evident in ritualized exchanges at tribal ceremonies such as a drum ceremony, which was criminalized until 1978.

The history of the rice season and its practices was related to me by Bob Shimek, based on his oral history research on wild rice with Lower Rice Lake elders. According to Bob's research, ricers from nine Anishinabek tribes, including White Earth, the nearby Red Lake Band, and, further afield, the Mille Lacs and Cass Lake Bands, gathered at Rice Lake in the months of September and October. In general, each family from the tribes was allowed to keep two to three bags of rice for subsistence needs. This would be about seventy-five pounds for a family of four to six, who might eat rice 150 to 200 days per year. After household needs were met, families were allowed to set aside a certain amount of the total harvest to trade for the other needs with white merchants from the surrounding towns. Such needs included frying pans, shotguns, and other food staples. The remaining surplus was ceremonially distributed to those who weren't able to rice for themselves (the very old) or who had had some trouble that year (those who were sick or injured). The ceremonial "giveaway" functioned as a way to ensure that no one went hungry. According to Shimek, this was an important function of food security in the community that required that everyone look out for one another and to know the needs of people in the community. Also, surplus was distributed via "gambling sticks," which Shimek says is another form of the gift economy. He says that the game ensured that "someone with five frying pans, for example, who only needed one, could make sure a frying pan got to someone who needed one."

During my time at White Earth, I repeatedly observed the gift economy in action, but most significantly in the months following the rice harvest on the reservation in 2010. A drum ceremony was held as the season ended, one of several key points of rice circulation. There are many stories about the origin of the drum, but one story has it that the drum is held by the tribe as a reminder of a gift from the Lakota. It was given to them in the 1800s in order to resolve cross-tribal conflict and to unite the two groups against the American military. The drum ceremonies, which are organized by the drum chiefs, are one important site of gifting and construction of knowledge, community, and identity.

Manoomin circulates at the event through an offering to the drum, through offerings to a new drum chief, through the singing of a "giveaway" song during which everyone gives someone else something (i.e., cloth, rice), and through the feast that follows the ceremony. The drum ceremonies and related tribal dances are significant ceremonies that are a frequent part of social life for the tribe. The circulation of *manoomin* between tribal members is a key source of food security and is a way that the giving practices that characterized the historic "rice camp" live on.

As Appadurai (1988) asserts, commodities appear when things pass through situations that construct them as something destined for sale. While *manoomin's* social place in the community is largely that of a gift, in the modern economy of the tribe, it is also a commodity. The rice is still harvested by hand and parched in locally run mills, in ways not terribly different from those used before colonial contact. However, now any extra not kept for the ricer's family is not distributed in the historic ways, through sharing and gambling at the rice camp. It is sold, either to the tribal council, which resells it to tribal members, or to the White Earth Land Recovery Project, which sells it on its website and through other outlets both on and off the reservation. As such, rice circulates as both gift and commodity, sometimes simultaneously, as some purchased rice may become a gift to an elder, who may trade it or give it away. My intention in relating the story of the gifting of *manoomin* is not to harken back in a nostalgic way to a simpler time but to understand how food security can work in anticapitalist ways, in places in which the state has willfully abandoned its role in providing for its people. The strategies used by the White Earth Tribe (and other tribes) are an adaptation to the commoditization process, which has consequences for the management of commonly held resources.

Lakes as Commons

Shimek also told me about the management practices that historically were incorporated into the rice camp. A few ricers came early to set up camp a month or so ahead of the rice harvest and to create a dam on the lake to raise the water levels so the rice could be easily harvested. A "Rice Council" composed of representatives from each tribe determined when the rice was ready to be harvested and how much could be taken. Ricers usually "seeded" the lake for the next year's crop by dropping grains into the water instead of the canoe, a practice that continues today. Shimek says that "the giving of wild rice to each other sustains our community, and it's not just limited to humans. We have to give back to the lake to ensure the crop next year." The dam was left in place to be washed away by the high water in the spring because *manoomin* needs the light and warmth of shallow waters to germinate in the spring. In spite of the

FIGURE 10. White Earth ricers selling freshly harvested rice to WELRP. (Author's photo)

intimate and interdependent knowledge of the needs of the ricing lakes held by Native ricers, management of lakes is currently overseen by the state Department of Natural Resources (DNR). According to other White Earth respondents, the number of lakes with rice in them off the reservations has declined since the state established authority over their management.

The DNR also polices the harvesting of rice on lakes off the reservation, in spite of 1855 treaty reserve rights that some Natives say grant them usufruct rights to the off-reservation lakes. The tribe regulates the rice and the hunting of game on the reservation but does not always observe the geopolitical boundaries that mark the limits of tribal territory now. In a widely followed but criminalized practice, Native ricers will also "seed" lakes off the reservation. According to the DNR, it is illegal to move aquatic species from one lake to another, so seeding off-reservation lakes, many of which used to have rice but do not now, is also illegal. Also, while it is legal for tribal members to rice on tribal land or on their own property without a permit from the state, it is not legal off the reservation. According to a Red Lake–enrolled member living on the White Earth Reservation in 2013, "Hardly any white guys rice, but still they don't want us to have it." He then related a story about how he was stopped at a gas station by a DNR official and asked for ricing permits on the basis of having a canoe and a push pole in his truck. He said he was eventually given a warning based on the canoe not having a state registration sticker, saying the DNR official "had to find something."

The 1855 claims to treaty rights are currently hotly disputed in northern Minnesota, and while settlements are being arranged (or not), the state DNR continues to harass ricers and fishers. Many people told me that the DNR's strategy is to issue citations but dismiss the cases in the state courts, because it's a federal dispute. So Natives are continuously harassed for asserting rights off the reservation even though their "violations" are rarely prosecuted. The citations are a strategy of harassment that poses intimidating barriers to Native ricers and costs them money and time in unnecessary legal entanglements. While anger and resentment about the barriers to asserting off-reservation subsistence rights abound, some argue that the seasonal and spatial management of common-pool resources is a necessary thing. Speaking in 2014 about the ongoing treaty rights disputes, a White Earth tribal member said, "Some of these young guys get all mad when they [are] fined by the tribe for fishing or hunting out of season. You can't just take whatever you want whenever you want. We have always regulated this one way or another. We have learned that if you don't, you will lose it" (Tommy). This signals a sensitivity to the losses of the past but also an awareness of the need for management—just not the centralized, enclosed forms of management favored by the modern liberal state.

Food sovereignty advocates are clear about the role of commoditization in the production of food insecurity and hunger. The enclosure of land and the privatization of management facilitate the commoditization process, which forces producers into consumptive instead of productive roles. In the case of the Anishinabek, the literal enclosure of people and resources on the reservation attempted to end noncapitalist modes of exchange and the social relationships that support them, with the predictable results of widespread food insecurity and hunger. This transition is incomplete, however, and the production of non-capitalist subjects persists through the ritualized exchange of *manoomin* and the ongoing management of the commons in spite of its criminalization. The persistence of these practices also contributes to the work of creating subjects and nonnormative ways of relating to food and others.

While the gift economy of *manoomin* has been disrupted by colonialism, racism, and genocide, a collective subjectivity based on the nonmonetary exchange and circulation of food in the interests of food security persists. The reciprocal or gift exchange of wild rice on the White Earth Reservation is a unique cultural economy that also functions as a powerful strategy of disobedience to state and market control of the food system. Gift exchanges also cannot be regulated or criminalized by the state because they are noncommodified exchanges. The gifting of food is an exchange that is not regulated or taxed, and it forms the basis for long-lasting interdependence between families and communities. In the absence of state intervention of any kind, neoliberal or otherwise, community-based solutions are required, and the White Earth Tribe has, through the persistence of previously criminalized practices, invoked traditions of harvesting and sharing rice as a form of food security. The tribal governance of resources constitutes a kind of autonomous zone through which tribal interests can (but do not always) trump the interests of capital. In a form of "sovereignty within sovereignty," these autonomous zones extend off the reservation when tribal members act on the right to rice for subsistence means in spite of resistance from the state.

The sustainable use of the lakes for ricing requires the creation of a social context of exchange that emphasizes collective decision making within and across tribes about yields and management of rice production. The forms of power that are invoked against the arguably illegal actions of the sovereign state, which accumulate through dispossession, are instructive examples for thinking through how food sovereigntists reconfigure ideas of power (through disobedience), economy (through acting on rights to subsistence and noncommodified food exchanges), and shared access to property through overlapping zones of authority (tribal, state, federal) over territory. The ongoing interest of the state in supporting commercial gain, against the needs and rights of tribal members for subsistence, suggests that there are very deep waters into which food sovereignty advocates must step to assert rights to food security. As the case studies in preceding chapters have shown, the state *permits* the process of capital accumulation. It does not necessarily act in the interests of social welfare, unless the generation of capital is assumed to generate collective goods. Until this calculus is changed, the process of accumulation of capital through dispossession will continue, and the only alternatives will be criminalized, contested and hidden in radical collectives characterized by relations of care.

CHAPTER SIX

Making Political Space for Life
Seeds and Permaculture

Men and women . . . do you not realize that the State is the worst enemy you
have? It is a machine that crushes you in order to sustain the ruling class, your
masters. . . . The State is the pillar of capitalism, and it is ridiculous to expect any
redress from it.

Emma Goldman, 1931

In April 2014, in honor of Earth Day, a seed library opened in the public library
in the town of Mechanicsburg, Pennsylvania. The library operates on the idea
that whoever takes seeds will grow them out and return to the library new seed
stock that is adapted to the local growing conditions at the end of the season.
The seed library accepted donations of seeds from gardeners (a total of sixty
local members at the time) and allowed others to borrow the seeds to plant. A
few months after the seed library opened, the librarians received a letter from
the Pennsylvania Department of Agriculture (PDA) that claimed they were in
violation of a 2004 Pennsylvania law called the Seed Act. Following the letter,
officials and lawyers from the PDA visited the library in an aggressive move
very likely intended to intimidate the librarians. The reasoning behind their
concern was that distribution of seeds, if not properly labeled, could lead to the
spread of noxious weeds or invasive species. A member of a Mechanicsburg
commission interviewed for a story in the local newspaper cited concerns about
"agri-terrorism" and is quoted as saying that "protecting and maintaining the
food sources of America is an overwhelming challenge" (Creason, 2014a). This
incident, and others like it, reflects a growing unease on the part of the public
over the sources of their food, as well as a growing paranoia on the part of the
state when it comes to autonomous food production.[1]

Because seeds are the self-replicating and self-organizing building blocks of
all life, it is axiomatic that food sovereignty cannot proceed without some form
of seed sovereignty. How seed sovereignty can be achieved in a context in which

the liberal state aggressively regulates and governs the biological basis of agricultural productivity is an important question for food sovereignty to tackle. In the case of the Mechanicsburg library, even though they were not selling the seeds, the law was interpreted in such a way that giving constituted selling. A process of negotiation between the PDA and the library resulted in a regulatory framework for the seed library that required it to accept only labeled packets of seeds (although what constitutes a label was not clear); loose seeds could be accepted only if they underwent testing by a laboratory authorized by the state. The PDA official quoted in a follow-up news article cited the regulatory mandate supporting the agency's actions, which requires it to "protect commerce" (Creason, 2014b).

The privatization of genomic material through the recent development of legislation that supports patents and intellectual property rights is an ongoing process of enclosing the commons for private gain. While seeds have always been a product of agriculture, because of their self-replicating nature they are also a key means of production, and they have only recently become seen as property (Kloppenburg, 2005; Aoki, 2003). Patents and intellectual property rights have solidified the power of multinational corporations in a project of capitalist expansion into agriculture that requires farmers to buy seeds at the beginning of the planting season, rather than save them from the previous year's harvest. Laws that, in the most generous light, were meant to protect the interests of inventors and plant breeders have been extended so far that now librarians cannot share a handful of seeds in a public space without being accused of engaging in criminal activities. Only the most cynical could believe that laws protecting plant breeders should be used to prevent the sharing of vegetable seeds among home gardeners. Only the most ignorant could enforce such a law on open-pollinated varieties.

Why is the state so interested in preventing the noncommercial exchange of seeds? The state's interest in protecting commerce is established in other chapters in this book, but how and why is giving in a mutualist exchange subject to the regulation that usually applies to commodities and monetized exchange? How would it be possible to avoid the regulatory frame of the state in any sort of organized way if even nonmonetary exchanges are considered commercial activities? What interest does the state have in establishing and enforcing this seemingly absurd and possibly legally indefensible position? In what follows, I outline the history of seed legislation in the United States as well as discuss how and why seeds are so important to both the state and food sovereignty. Following that, I outline how a theory of postcapitalist politics can inform radically collective approaches to food production. I conclude by discussing a few examples of solutions to seed sovereignty that are proposed by activists and offering some insights into the way sociocultural realties are brought into being through these practices.

Seeds and Power

Since its inception, the U.S. government has encouraged the importation of plant material from other countries and has dedicated state agencies to this task (Kloppenburg, 2005; Fowler, 1994). The USDA was responsible for the development and free distribution of seeds until the 1920s. The agency ended its role in public seed projects after decades of intense lobbying pressure from the American Seed Trade Association (ASTA) on behalf of private plant breeders, who wanted more market share (Aoki, 2003).[2] The USDA purchased seed from private breeders, but the public seed program and the ability of farmers to save seeds kept private seed businesses from realizing large profits. Legislation passed following the disbanding of public seed programs criminalized the saving or sharing of plant genomic material, enabling private companies to assume the role of providing seeds to the public (Mascarenhas and Busch, 2006). The development of hybrid seeds and a variety of court cases in the last half of the twentieth century solidified multinational control over the supply of seed to farmers.

The coordination between state and capital to develop higher yielding seeds, also known as the Green Revolution, was a project of modernization and industrialization in agriculture. Commodity production is the foundation of economic development, and the United States used its prodigious agricultural power and wealth to develop as an industrial powerhouse throughout the nineteenth and twentieth centuries. At the same time, farmers were enrolled in circuits of capital by the enclosure of germplasm, which was once thought to be a "product of nature," and therefore not patentable. Legislation and the development of hybrids solved what Marx identified as the "recalcitrant" nature of agriculture. Seeds, because they self-replicate, have resisted commodification, since once "a seed was sold, the means of reproducing the seed went with it" (Aoki, 2003: 265). Unlike open-pollinated varieties, hybrid seeds do not "breed true" generation after generation, meaning that they will not express the same characteristics, including their increased yields, if saved. Hybrid seeds and the legal protection of patents make the commodification of seeds possible through technical (i.e., hybrids) and legal (i.e., patents) means.

Multinational corporations maintain control over their investment in the development of hybrid seeds (although much of the fundamental research on plant genetics has been done by the public sector) and expect to profit from it by developing hybrid seeds. As such, plant varieties are developed in several highly political and "noninnocent" ways (van Dooren, 2008). First, plant genomes used in basic research are often the "indigenous varieties" developed by farmers. In the appropriation of this research, the genomic material in seeds is transformed from "fixed capital into liquid capital" (Roy, 2014: 143). Second, the politics around genetically modified crops are less about concerns related to health and safety regarding transgenic seeds and more about political economic decisions about what food crops to market and where. Third, the justifications for investment in agrotechnologies that are related to food security and development are partial truths distributed to get political buy-in and do not tell the whole story. The use of plant material to make hybrid varieties that are marketed back to farmers as "improved" enrolls them in global capital in ways that may not necessarily be in their interests (Kloppenburg, 2010).

While crop and soil scientists argue in favor of hybrid and genetically modified technologies and their role in combating hunger, social scientists generally agree that traditional seed varieties and local seed exchange networks are essential for maintaining agrobiodiversity and peasant livelihoods (Kloppenburg, 2010; Rhoades and Nazarea, 1999; Zimmerer, 2003). For example, Zimmerer (2003) found that multicommunity and intracommunity networks of seed flows enhanced plants' adaptation to local environmental conditions more than did single-site seed production and distribution practices. The continued use and development of farmer varieties was especially key in an increasingly neoliberal environment in Peru, where state subsidies for the development and distribution of hybrid varieties is in decline. Similarly, Kloppenburg (2010) argues that "bioprospecting" in genomic material is accumulation through dispossession, which calls for legal and scientific scrutiny as a dubiously ethical practice. In his view, the patenting of life forms in seeds undermines the livelihoods of food producers; he calls for plant-breeding methods that keep the information about the genome freely available to the public, in what he refers to as "open-source" plant breeding.

Patents, TRIPS, and Seed Acts

Legal protection for intellectual property related to plant varieties did not extend to seed saving for replanting or to food crops until very recently. This new development emerged as a result of a lawsuit between Monsanto and a Mississippi farmer who saved seeds in spite of signing Monsanto's "Technology Agreement" that states that farmers cannot save seeds. The farmer, McFarling, argued that the seed-saving provision in the Plant Variety Protection law in the United States, which granted exemptions to farmers saving for replanting, protected his right to save seeds. The court ruled against him in 2000, opening the door to new restrictions on seed saving, such as those that have been used to shut down vegetable seed libraries (Blakeney, 2011). Aoki (2003) calls this the "market enclosure" of genomes, which is supported by the World Trade Organization Agreement on Trade-Related Aspects of Intellectual Property Rights (TRIPS), which set the requirements for legal protections on intellectual property, including patents on plant varieties. Aoki argues that the market capture of plant genetic information and the policy measures that support it do not bode well for the "continued health of local, subsistence farming practices premised on the gift economies of traditional agricultural communities" (257).

The situation does not bode well because of the way in which producers—even large-scale industrial producers like McFarling—are enrolled in circuits of capital; the legislation affects even those who are not enrolled. Another case, *Monsanto Canada v. Percy Schmeiser*, is an excellent example of the primacy of intellectual property over the rights of any agriculturalist—even those who do not use or buy patent-protected seeds or sign technology agreements. Schmeiser did not purchase Monsanto's glyphosate-resistant canola to plant on his Canadian farm, and he claims that genetic pollution from neighboring crops contaminated his farm. At the end of a prolonged legal battle, during which Schmeiser proclaimed his innocence, the Canadian Supreme Court ruled that even if Schmeiser did not purchase the seed, he had "used" it without a license, in violation of patent law. Aoki (2003) calls this the "apotheosis of germplasm as a commodity," in which the "means of (re)production have now been separated from the commodity form" (297). In other words, even seeds that are not protected by patents are subject to the same legal protections granted to patented varieties. As such, all seeds must be purchased through formal markets.

Kloppenburg (2010) identifies this as "accumulation by dispossession" (cf. Harvey, 2003), which is, according to Marx (1867/1977), the alienation of the worker from the means of production. In this case, the farmer is divorced from the means of production, that of the self-replicating nature of germplasm. Opposing this process has been a key point of resistance for the world's subsistence farmers as well as activists dedicated to keeping open the seed commons. Exploiting loopholes in existing trade agreements or circumventing patent laws have met with little success, largely because, as Kloppenburg (2010) argues, intellectual property rights were established to protect corporate interests. Cooperative, collective, or collaborative approaches to seed development and distribution undermine corporate control of the commodity form of seeds. The investment in both legislation and scientific breeding to control the more "recalcitrant" aspects of agricultural production will not be relinquished easily.

The so-called Seed Act invoked in the closure of the seed library in Pennsylvania is a further extension of the control of information and distribution of seeds. The act calls for "adding provisions relating to the labeling, sale and distribution of seed; [and] creating a licensing requirement for all seed distributors" and specifies penalties for noncompliance, including up to ninety days in jail. On the surface the Seed Act appears to be a well-intentioned piece of legislation designed to protect growers (of commodity and garden crops alike) from purchasing unviable seed from vendors who have not been certified by the state to sell seed. Digging deeper, the language in the act makes it clear that the only seed that the state will allow to be sold is that which has passed through the industrialized commodity seed system. The licensing requirements are not onerous, but the stipulations for certification of seeds, including guarantees of germination rates, are not something the average seed saver or even a small businessperson could manage.

Legislation similar to the Pennsylvania Seed Act is on the books in several states, and given ASTA's history in shaping legislation, it should not be a surprise that the organization is behind the push to harmonize legislation across state lines. According to its website, ASTA's legislative agenda is to "ensure that state regulations relating to the seed industry remain consistent between the states. This allows for smoother interstate trade, equalized competition, and elimination of unnecessary, duplicative and burdensome regulations" (ASTA, 2014).

In addition to couching its agenda in terms of facilitating interstate trade, ASTA also advocates for preemption of federal law through a network of state laws that follow its guidelines, rather than the federal ones. The organization opposes labeling of transgenic crops and asserts that the lack of protection of intellectual property when it comes to seed will undermine the ability of plant breeders to develop varieties to "feed the world" (ASTA, 2014). It also should not be a surprise that ASTA's membership is primarily composed of seed companies.

Kloppenburg (2010) champions the General Public License for Plant Germplasm, which is a kind of open-source plant breeding in which a new commons for germplasm can be held and protected as a form of seed sovereignty that protects small-scale producers from the problems of patents and intellectual property rights of corporations. But if facilitating the saving of any seed that isn't certified, no matter who bred it, will land a librarian in jail for ninety days, this doesn't seem to do much in the face of the new legislative barriers enacted at the state level. The legal and technical means of forcing any food producer into circuits of capital are formidable forces to oppose. Opting out, resisting, or otherwise circumventing the system to achieve seed sovereignty will take considerable imagination and determination. Perhaps clues lie in the self-replicating and regenerative nature of seed, which by its own mechanisms resists privatization and enclosure by capitalism.

State Capitalism and Its Agonists

While scholarly attention to the collusion of the state with capital to subjugate a population is a relatively recent intervention in the social sciences, critiques of the state as a tool of capitalism are nothing new among labor activists. For more than a century, anarchists have voiced criticisms of both the communist and the liberal state, with little recognition of their position by social scientists. In geography, a small resurgence of interest in anarchism happened in the late 1970s, with more sustained interest gathering steam recently in what might be called a "radical turn" (Valentine, 2005). This comes after a period in which the "Left" has leaned further to the middle of the political spectrum by embracing liberal, market-based reforms. According to Clough and Blumberg (2012), "perhaps it is time to consider a Left politics that embraces liberty, autonomy, self-sufficiency and the common over the old shibboleths of the state, the public, and Left vanguardism" (348). This resurgence of interest in anarchist geographies draws scholarly attention to the ways in which activists can "prefigure politics" by working to territorialize autonomous political space within existing institutional structures (Ince, 2012).

QUESTIONING AUTHORITY

Rather than looking backward with a nostalgic view to labor struggles in the past, as is commonly assumed, anarchist social theory looks forward to a post-neoliberal future (White & Williams, 2012). Unlike communism or socialism, which privilege class-based struggles and often appeal to the state for protections and rights, anarchism foments resistance to hierarchy in any form in all spaces (Breitbart, 1978). According to Clough and Blumberg (2012), anarchist social theory and action are dedicated to understanding how best to "question and challenge all forms of domination" in society and the economy (337). The central principles of anarchism are "mutual aid, solidarity, self-determination and individual freedom that is socially supported" (Clough & Blumberg, 2012: 337). Graeber (2009) also identifies "autonomy, voluntary association, self-organization, direct democracy and mutual aid" as central organizing principles of anarchism (105). In short, anarchism is a political project to foster cooperation and collectivism specifically focused on efforts to reorganize the provisioning of housing, food, and clothing (Kropotkin, 1907).

After the Haymarket Affair of 1886 in Chicago, anarchism has been negatively associated with violence and attempts at state overthrow in most popular imaginations. Examination of the foundational writings on anarchism, however, reveal something more threatening to the state and capital than riots, bombs, and violence ever could be. Anarchism posits the radical idea that human societies can be self-organizing and self-determined and they have no need of overarching authority to organize the provision of basic needs. In fact, anarchism asserts that hierarchical forms of society perpetuate inequality and the maldistribution of resources, upon which capitalism thrives. Anarchist scholars such as Emma Goldman, whose quote opens this chapter, have long argued that state and capital are mutually co-constituted and are also mutually perpetuating. As such, appeals to the state for rights, as illustrated elsewhere in this volume, may only end in "capture" by the state. Ince (2012) argues that an "anarchist critique of the interlinked system of capital and authority . . . opens up our spatial and political imaginations to radical alternatives" (1646).

Ince (2012) asserts that anarchist imaginaries of autonomy and nonhierarchical politics rest on a re/deterritorializing process characterized by "diverse territorial practices" (1650). These territorial strategies are premised on what he argues are the two most salient characteristics of anarchism to contemporary political struggles: the critique of all forms of authority and "prefigurative" politics. In a direct parallel to the narratives of food sovereignty, contemporary anarchism prioritizes the concept of socially supported "autonomy," as opposed to "freedom," in its critique of authority (Garland, 2010; Ince, 2012). Prefigurative politics stresses building new political futures within the existing institutional frames of contemporary society. This approach rests on the notion that revolution or overthrow simply reproduces the unequal structures that were resisted in the first place (Graeber, 2009). Prefigurative politics assume that social transformation is never complete and that society is constantly in the process of "becoming" (Ince, 2012; cf. Massey, 2005).

BECOMING AUTONOMOUS THROUGH LOVE

Autonomy does not imply state overthrow or revolution; rather, it suggests that people have the "capacity for cooperative and rational organic social harmony" (Garland, 2010: 11). Autonomous practice implies nonhierarchal and equal social relationships that are inconsistent with the "violence of capitalism" (i.e., wage labor, commodification, or the value process). According to anarchist social theory, the achievement of autonomy as a "non-exploitative social relation in which human beings' capacity for freedom and cooperation is recognized and encouraged" (Garland, 2010: 13) can and must be achieved within, and perhaps between, the state structures that frustrate such efforts. Hardt and Negri (2009) argue that there is no autonomous place to which we can retreat. Rather, the transformation of society must be done with the tools available to us in everyday life in the spaces of the present. Hébert and Mincyte (2014) argue that it is not enough to practice autonomy; the way in which resources are extracted, valued, and exchanged must be rethought as well.

Carlsson and Manning (2010) identify the concept of "nowtopia" as an example of resistance to the "basic violence at the heart of capitalist production: the process of turning creative, useful human activity into abstract labor dedicated to producing value for people other than those who labor" (926). Carlsson and Manning assert that everyone has reason to combat capitalism and that "nowtopia" consists of work done "for social and ecological reasons and not for the proliferation of capital" (928). They identify community gardens, guerrilla gardening, and permaculture as quintessential examples of the way in which unpaid labor poses epistemological challenges to capital through "life-affirming, self-emancipating behaviors" (925). The "recalcitrance" of agricultural production, which, through living, self-replicating things, resists the logic of capital, becomes subordinated to it through patents, contract farming, and substitution of inputs for ecological services. Resistance to capitalism as "nowtopia" includes reconnecting labor to products and allowing life to do work that is not subject to valuation as a commodity.

Nowtopians participate in the production of actual things (i.e., food, bi-cycles), and also in the construction of new economic subjectivities. Gibson-Graham (2006) identify this as the process of "resubjectivation"—"the mobiliza-tion and transformation of desires, the cultivation of capacities, and the making of new identifications" (xxxvi). They also point out that resisting the production of authority via state and capital requires practicing new ways of "being in com-mon" (86). hooks (2006), in her essay "Love as the Practice of Freedom," in-vokes this sentiment as a "love ethic," in which systems of oppression and capi-talist accumulation and hierarchical ways of relating are transformed through love. She writes with reference to a collective, versus an individual, struggle to end domination of that which hurts us:

> This is why we desperately need an ethic of love to intervene in our self-centered
> longing for change. Fundamentally, if we are only committed to an improvement in
> that politic of domination that we feel leads directly to our individual exploitation
> or oppression, we not only remain attached to the status quo but act in complicity
> with it, nurturing and maintaining those very systems of domination. Until we are
> all able to accept the interlocking, interdependent nature of systems of domination
> and recognize specific ways each system is maintained, we will continue to act in
> ways that undermine our individual quest for freedom and collective liberation
> struggle.

Anarchist and feminist social theory also invoke love and care as central organizing principles for transformative social change. Kropotkin (1907), a pre-mier anarchist thinker who argued for the abolishment of waged labor and the re-creation of the commons, opens his chapter on food in *The Conquest of Bread* with this statement: "To attain a new end, new means are required" (47). What this new end requires is the production, maintenance, and sustenance of an ecological or social commons, in which "all is for all" (Kropotkin, 1907: 14). As hooks (2006) puts it simply, "[In] choosing love we also choose to live in com-munity, and that means we do not have to change by ourselves" (248).

Permaculture as Production Model

When I embarked on ten months of research to investigate the practice and politics of food sovereignty in a variety of field sites around the world, I knew something of permaculture from my work with activists in Athens prior to my departure. I was surprised, however, by the way in which permaculture per-vaded food sovereignty narratives everywhere I went. Permaculture was a con-stant narrative theme in my fieldwork, beginning with my first conversation with an activist in Belgium about Fukoaka's *One Straw Revolution*, reappearing again in the wide use of twelve-crop polycultures in rural India, and ending with the harvesting of *manoomin* (native wild grain) in northern Minnesota.[3] Even the family with whom I stayed in the Dominican Republic for another project (Trauger, 2014) cultivated the kind of urban food forest integrated with small livestock that is common throughout the Caribbean. I'll present an example in this chapter of permaculture practices in Athens, which is by no means representative of the wide variety of permaculture practices that exist, but it is the community with which I have the longest and closest ties, which helps provide the deepest contextualization of permaculture as an ecological and social practice. I have worked with the permaculture group in Athens from its inception in 2009, and I participated in the construction of a perennial garden in a right-of-way near a stream. I also worked with them to establish a community kitchen used by an artist cooperative in an adjacent building. The building also housed a bicycle cooperative and is the weekly distribution point for an online farmers market for which I also volunteer.[4]

PERMANENT AGRICULTURE

Permaculture is, in one sense, a design-based planting and cropping system that relies on perennial herbaceous plants and trees, which bear nuts and fruits as well as provide other useful products, such as medicine, forage, fencing, shade, habitat for beneficial organisms, and aesthetic pleasure. Permaculture is, however, much more than just a cropping system. It is, according to a practitioner in Athens, a "transformative agricultural practice that focuses on cultural change. The word 'permaculture' comes from fusing the words 'permanent' and 'agriculture,' but it's also about the cultural changes will have to take place to make that happen" (Ethan). Permaculturalists envision an agri-culture so reliant on agro-ecological principles that the majority of food could be provided through "food forests" (Hemenway, 2009). A food forest has multiple levels of plants filling a variety of ecological functions, including nutrient cycling. It consequently has a dramatically higher yield per acre but also requires an integrated crop-livestock system that provides far higher caloric value and a far wider nutritional spectrum per acre than any other cropping system.

For example, according to Martin Crawford, a noted permaculturalist in the UK, sweet chestnut trees can yield up to two tons per acre, which is the equivalent of an average yield for organic wheat. Sweet chestnuts have a nearly identical caloric profile to grains, with greater nutritional value and health benefits and higher yield per acre with far fewer inputs. According to Molnar, Kahn, Ford, Funk, and Funk (2013) a small city with a population of forty-seven thousand could obtain about two hundred calories per person per day from walnuts grown on only 2.5 acres. When tree crops are integrated with small-scale livestock and annual and perennial fruits and vegetables, permaculture shows the most promise to withstand ecological crises, growing populations, and economic pressures that increase the cost of inputs, including and especially seeds. In addition, seeds are rarely required as inputs in a permaculture system, as most crops are perennial. Annuals can also be selectively limited to those that will self-sow. Clyde Yeats, a permaculturalist in Athens, calls permaculture "a design system for regenerative human habitats." He goes on to say that "to me it's about how are we going to design ourselves and our environment to work in harmony so that we can stick around this planet for a long time."

This has more than a little liberatory potential in a context in which seed stock is controlled by multinational corporations and seed banking is increasingly criminalized. What I found as I investigated permaculture and the politics around it is that permaculture is beneficial not so much because it offers a seedless solution to the problems of modernist agriculture (although it does do that) but because it also focuses on cultural change toward nonhierarchal forms of interaction within the existing system. Clyde observes that Bill Mollison and David Holgren, who were architects of modern permaculture, realized that their work wasn't just about agriculture. It was about adaptation of cultural systems as well. Clyde says, "It is a WIDE reaching thing, this idea of permaculture living, and the principles can be applied to everything that we do. It is conscious living modeled on . . . ancient and long-standing horticultural systems and probably spiritual systems too. It is a modern amalgamation of what . . . was working for people before grain and commodity agriculture moved other horticultural systems out of the way."

Clyde runs a permaculture gardening business in Athens, and at the time of my second interview with him, he felt defeated after trying to establish edible gardens on a wider scale. He identified the perennial problems of time and money as obstacles to a deeper engagement with permaculture for most people, but he also signaled his persistence and engagement with what anarchists would call "prefigurative politics." He said, "What I see is that there's a lot of metanarrative about capitalism and consumerism and needing to change it, but without recognizing that those are the systems that we are in and working with."

THE PEOPLE'S PERENNIAL PEACE GARDEN

In 2009 a University of Georgia faculty member in landscape architecture worked with Clyde and the Athens Permaculture Group to design a rain garden called the People's Perennial Peace Garden (PPP) for the Tanyard Creek watershed. The creek is one of the few remaining open water bodies in the metropolitan area of Athens, and the portions of it that are still above ground are exposed to road runoff, erosion, and infestation with invasive species, such as kudzu. The result of the project was a multispecies perennial garden with fruit trees and herbs interspersed with vegetables and flowers. Clyde, who led much of the implementation by organizing work parties, said of the design, "There is

FIGURE 11. View of the People's Perennial Peace Garden in spring from the parking lot. (Author's photo)

a scree wall going down to the creek. That's now the low point that we've constructed, so what water-harvesting devices don't accumulate, you know, heavy rains, it'll overflow there and now instead of just causing a gully again it's going to go over some big pieces of sidewalk we salvaged from a construction project a couple blocks up the street. We have a great portfolio that we want to show the city to say, 'Look how legit this is!'"

A gardener who cultivates a community garden on property belonging to the historic Hill First Baptist Church on the other side of the creek (figure 11) helped with the planting, as did a group of homeless men who live in the neighborhood and work in and eat food from the church's community garden.

The garden is based on the idea that food should be free and that gardens should be accessible to all, regardless of who maintains them or how they are cultivated. Permaculture lends itself well to implementing this kind of vision since the labor requirements for a perennial garden are minimal after the initial installation. In the case of the PPP, students, activists, and permaculture group members contributed the labor and materials. In addition to the plants being mostly crowdsourced, a dozen fruit trees were donated anonymously. The idea that food should be free came up frequently in meetings of the permaculture group, and Clyde had a particularly inspiring idea for planting perennials throughout Athens. He said,

I had this idea a few days ago and I'm calling it freedom trees. Freedom trees! Where the harvest from the tree is free to the public, it might be and it's a free tree, nobody owns it. And I want to have "plant a tree for freedom" day. Turn it into this big public spectacle, like Arbor Day. You can come and pick up your tree then and then we'll give demonstrations throughout the day on how to plant it. There's food growing out there, people know what it is, and they're paying attention to it and they might care about it, they might steward it. And if we, like, plant a hundred trees, how many pounds of food? How many calories is that going to produce in five years? I don't know. A lot. And it's free. There's food security right there!

In another interview he articulated that he wanted there "to be so much food that people could eat off of the land, like what if there were so many blueberries scattered throughout the landscape, that no one ever felt it necessary to protect or claim their blueberry bush from being harvested by somebody else?!" These are the new means for new ends that Kropotkin writes about, built on the philosophy that "all should be for all."

The city was largely helpful and cooperative with the PPP, although no one believes that the city would encourage the cultivation of fruit trees that would drop fruit on sidewalks. And in fact, until 2015 a city ordinance actually forbade the cultivation of food crops and the keeping of chickens and bees in the city. It is widely known that home gardens are largely ignored by code enforcement officials and urban livestock violations are pursued only if complaints are filed. Community gardens are exempt from the ordinance, but most have been developed on the grounds of current or former schools and churches. Because the PPP was developed in a riparian zone it was technically in a right-of-way, a legal gray area, and since maintenance of the water body was work that no longer had to be done by the city, the garden was tacitly supported by city and planning officials.

The permaculture activists who implemented, maintained, and use the garden see it as an asset to the community, particularly since it has been connected to a kitchen. They see it as a way to provide food for free and to forge connections through the growing, cooking, and sharing of food. Ethan said of the promise of the kitchen, "We're social creatures, that's what we do, we help each other out. And food is like the center of that in so many cultures, we're all sharing food. Eating together, that's what we do. . . . But to me, this is nature, too. It's an internal nature, a social nature. . . . So cultivating that sort of deep nature ourselves is first, rather than the other way of thinking of an external authority with transactional ways of thinking" (Ethan).

This statement echoes the anarchist emphasis on nonhierarchical modes of relating and also the deep-seated conviction that, given the chance, people are capable of cooperating and caring for each other. All of the projects the permaculture group and its members support also happen within the context of existing social, economic, and political structures with an eye toward or hope for social transformation. The goal is not to change things. Change is the goal.

Master Plan

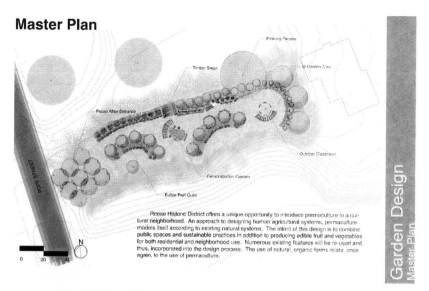

FIGURE 12. Map of the People's Perennial Peace Garden. (Used with permission from Sungkyung Lee)

Clyde articulated this when I asked him whether permaculture has the potential to change agricultural production toward producing a more just and secure food supply. He was pessimistic about permaculture's agricultural capacity to make change but articulated hope when it came to permaculture's transformative potential to work within and change the existing system, because it focuses on productive, positive change, rather than revolution or destruction.

> If the system that permaculture proposes is the one that we want (whoever we are) then it can't just throw itself up as an alternative. But it—the people involved in permaculture who are trying to create this alternative reality—have got to get in and work within the other system to transform it because . . . there's a lot of inertia built into that system. There's a lot of money and a lot of power, and I know that for me, I can't engage in destroying that system but if I think there's an alternative system to it that I'd prefer, then my action has to be: where can I find fertile ground to plant these alternative seeds to being a player in a process of transformation, rather than [participating in] destruction and then rebuilding?

In the beginning and in the end, permaculture, like anarchism, is not about overthrow or even a direct challenge to the system but the transformation of relationships within an existing system. The relationships that permaculture aims to change are those characterized by selfishness and greed, values supported and encouraged by capitalism.

"OUR CULTURE IS DEEPLY TRAUMATIZED"

Other permaculture activists were not so sanguine about working within the structures of capitalism and consumption and identified both as at the root of problems of hunger, food insecurity, and inequality. One activist—who at the time also ran an educational center that taught children (and adults) about ecology, wilderness, and survival skills—spoke frequently in our meetings about how the way in which people interact reflects the way in which capitalism shapes the economy. He said, "In Western society, people are interacting with both the natural world and the people from a transactional standpoint, which means I'll interact with someone if I'm going to get something out of it, they're commodities to me, basically, the transaction. Slavery, for instance, is a transactional relationship between people. There's still a lot of that kind of way of being in the world that dominates the world" (Ethan).

In an interview with Ethan, during which we discussed the development of a community kitchen as a place in which those transactional relationships could be transformed to create a way of being that fosters resilience and the ability to withstand, he described what he called "shocks" to society that undermine our capacity to provide for ourselves and each other. Speaking about the community kitchen we were developing, he said, "So what I want to see in this place is a shift to what some of my mentors call relational interactions with people, which is based on relationships. And there's transactions within that relationship, obviously, but it's more about the long-term relationship and a mutual concern for everyone's well-being in the community. And the term that I like to think of is community resilience, we're building resilience" (Ethan).

Another activist, the founder of the bicycle cooperative in the building, added, "I personally believe that we're all deeply traumatized human beings. I think our culture is deeply traumatized. I think that we have no concept of how deeply traumatized we are. We're so fucked up, we don't know we're fucked up." He linked this trauma to Ethan's description of relationships that are built around transactional modes of interacting. He argued that it takes a kind of "experience every now and again in our lives that somehow blow[s] us out of our trap and let[s] us really wrap our consciousness around it. And then [we can] use that experience to kind of . . . figure out how we get through this" (Don).

Don said he wants to create and nurture a place in the community where people can be supported in realizing "the situation we're in and how bad it is and then to have some way to get out of this program that we're running that we don't even know is running. I want people to be able to share it with people who are meaningful to them and have a deep sense of trust that we've developed over meals and cooking." After saying this he held up a bandaged hand and demonstrated how the community kitchen created an opportunity to connect, care, and heal. He had cut his hand while chopping vegetables for our shared meal, and Clyde had grabbed some yarrow (an herb with coagulant properties) from the permaculture garden that he had planted next to the nearby creek. "So, like, that right there, [the yarrow] just served to heal, it's a medicinal plant. So creating that free food with free plants makes it available to everyone who needs it" (Don). Ethan followed Don's comments by saying, "It seems like it's all about relationships to me. Its relationship to a plant, that plant has a relationship to land, that we helped create. So I think as human beings we have the joy of being architects to our reality."

If we take seriously the emphasis on relationships and egalitarianism that these permaculture activists continually see as vital to their work, it is possible to see that food sovereignty isn't just about food, just like seed sovereignty isn't really about seeds. It's about relationships, and changing the relationships that support and perpetuate the "deeply traumatized" culture of "transactional relating" upon which capitalist social relations exist. As anarchists of all kinds and many others have pointed out, the problem of capitalism is not that it fetishizes markets but that it asks us to operate from the worst aspects of ourselves: privileging private interests, selfishness, and competition and believing that private gain is a public good. In this context people are not encouraged to explore the possible pre-sents and futures that cooperation, mutual aid, and care for others can produce. Anarchists and permaculturalists, using almost the same words, articulate the ethos of change from within existing structures through the cultivation of new, collective ways of relating.

The problem of capitalism as articulated by the permaculturalists in this chapter has to do with privatization, including the way in which relationships are reduced to transactions. They articulate a need to find an alternative to the privatization and enclosure of agricultural land, food production, and distribu-tion. In a direct echo of anarchists, leaders of the Athens Permaculture Group firmly believe that food should be free and that "all should be for all" (Kro-potkin, 1907). Knowing the institutional constraints on implementing such a vision, however, including ordinances banning food production, the inertia of the existing system, and the unpopularity of food-producing plants in the city, they articulate a "prefigurative" politics of working with the city to change sen-sitive riparian zones for permaculture, leveraging access to privately held space to open it to the community through a kitchen and cultivating shifts in values through education and outreach to both the public and the city.

The garden and the kitchen are examples of spaces that reflect a shift in values and subjectivities that could change the system from within. But in spite of their autonomy, these spaces and the affordable housing and community centers in the neighborhood compete with "development." Both the garden and the kitchen are in a historic district along a main artery into the town, and as Athens grows, it is only a matter of time before the garden and building are demolished and replaced with chain restaurants. The historic truck farmers marketplace that hosted the Athens Locally Grown market was demolished to make way for development just up the street in 2012, which prompted the move to the building with the garden and kitchen. This means that the values shift also needs to accompany a different kind of governing—one that protects and values enclaves of cooperation. That such governance will not arise is mostly a foregone conclusion, but this is the political work of food sovereignty: to create radically collective spaces of autonomy and protect them through democratic processes.

In terms of seeds, Kloppenburg's (2010) "open-source plant breeding" is not enough to stem the tide of corporate influence over the seed supply. Kloppenburg's model still works within a capitalist system and only frees up knowledge exchange between plant breeders. It does not distribute or share germplasm among farmers or gardeners, nor does it change the facts that seed banking is criminalized in many places and many seeds are privatized through hybrid technologies or patents. The need for seed sovereignty calls for different kinds of action: first, a policy response that recognizes, values, and protects the capacity to cooperate and share. Common Dreams, a progressive online news source, outlines a template for legislation that would amend the current seed laws to protect farmers and gardeners. The template explains that seed libraries should be exempt from all "licensing, testing, labeling, and other requirements of . . . various seed laws." In addition, people should be granted the legal protection to engage in noncommodified exchanges without fear of bogus charges, fines, and jail time justified by "protecting commerce." This effort would recognize the capacity of people to practice subsidiarity—decision making that doesn't rely on hierarchal authority. While not nearly accomplishing all of the work that is required for food sovereignty, this is a small start in freeing up the food system from corporate control, which leaves us all at the mercy of the state and the capital interests that are parasitic upon it.

CONCLUSION

Love as a Radically Collective Practice

> A society founded on serfdom is in keeping with absolute monarchy; a society
> based on the wage system and the exploitation of the masses by capitalists finds its
> political expression in parliamentarianism. But a free society, regaining possession
> of the common inheritance, must seek in free groups and free federations of
> groups, a new organization, in harmony with the new economic phase of history.
> **Peter Kropotkin, 1907: 43**

Without doubt, the political aims of food sovereignty envision a "new economic
phase of history," one that is characterized largely by limits on corporate power,
achieved either through legislation, self-governing, or civil disobedience. In the
United States, democracy originally was based on the principle of free government (not free markets), which included significant limits on the power of
corporations, such as restriction of the scope and scale of their operations, limits to their longevity, and restrictions on their contributions to political campaigns. Over time these restrictions have eroded and morphed into corporate
rights, including the nearly unfathomable right to status as a person. One of
the many battles food sovereignty wages is against corporate capital. The problem that corporate control poses for freedom and security is not its control of
markets but that it traffics in competition, selfishness, and narrow measures
of success and abundance and that it forces those values on us, through territorial, state-based policies. Corporations, which dominate so much of modern
economic life, have no capacity for generosity, cooperation, or love for others.
It's time—past time—to usher in a new era of relating through our politics and
our economy.

Food sovereignty, in all of its forms outlined in this book, is positioned as a
biopolitical and sometimes geopolitical struggle over power and control in the
food system. The battlefield is as much discursive as it is material, but the raids,
fines, arrests, and demolitions experienced by farmers, seed savers, ricers, and

gardeners outlined in this book demonstrate that the struggle is real and worthy of attention. Food sovereignty also constitutes a definitional challenge to the state- and capital-dominated transnational food regime. It calls into question the priorities of corporations and the way they shape values and subjectivities in society. Food sovereignty also offers alternative ways of governing, relating, and growing food that are instructive in face of Holt-Giménez and Shattuck's (2011) admonitions against mission creep back to alternative food networks. This book engages with the discursive and the material to articulate the way in which food sovereignty is new and different from what came before it.

I intend this book to contribute to the development of what McKittrick (2006) calls "more humanly workable geographies" (xii). My aim has been not only to excavate and shed light on marginal, invisible, and illicit practices in the food system but to cocreate what McKittrick calls an "interpretive alterable world; rather than a transparent and knowable world" (xiii). Space does work that is frequently neither acknowledged nor even comprehended and creates new possibilities. In the struggle to bring new geographies of power to the food system, activists mobilize and recast space and territory, resulting in the criminalization of subjects. McKittrick writes, "Our environment, our cities, our towns . . . continually render the world around us as simply given. . . . To challenge [existing structures] can be a very threatening act: it is punishable, erasable and oppositional" (145). According to Patel (2005), food sovereignty also has the potential to create "different kinds of people"; in so doing, it also creates new kinds of spaces, pregnant with possibility for a more "humanly workable" future.

Knowing and Doing Food Sovereignty

Food sovereignty does not appear in a political vacuum, nor is its emergence the result of recent events. The process of accumulation through dispossession, enclosure of common lands, and privatization of all the means of production in agriculture has been a centuries-long project of modernity. Food sovereignty emerges in the contemporary era as a political tipping point, perhaps a point of no return, in response to the scope and scale of immiseration under capitalist so-called development. Food sovereignty narratives directly oppose the commoditization process, which deepens capitalist social relations into autonomous zones of production and erodes the capacity for self-sufficiency of people everywhere. The criminalization of alternatives is the last move and tightens the screws on activists, farmers, gardeners, seed savers, and Natives alike. It also reveals the degree to which the liberal state works to further the accumulation of capital in the private sector.

Food sovereignty narratives frequently frame the problem of food insecurity as a problem of capital and situate the state as the protector of and guarantor of rights to farmers. This book grapples with the tension that arises as claims to rights from the state or suprastate are contradicted by desires for freedom from the power and influence of capital. If the liberal state is the guarantor of rights, then demands for autonomy must contend with the way in which the state grants rights to corporations and reserves the right to regulate commerce, often in the interests of private capital. In this book I have engaged with this central contradiction by reading political theories of liberal sovereignty to explain why freedom from state-backed corporate control of the food system cannot be realized through appeals to the state alone. For this reason, I don't have a great deal of hope that food sovereigntists will succeed in their goals, but I do believe that the process is what matters and that the process is what is needed now. But first, some thoughts on how we know and do food sovereignty.

In chapter 2 I discussed different framings of food sovereignty among a variety of voices in what people increasingly call a "movement." For some in the Global North, food sovereignty means removing state oversight of food production and distribution. Joel Salatin is a vocal and popular critic of the state and the way it impedes his ability to produce and sell food on a small scale. Much of the rhetoric from Nyéléni about political autonomy and freedom from trade policies resonates with this libertarian framing of food sovereignty. This reactionary and self-interested interpretation fails to explain many of the cases of food sovereignty action that I observed in my research, for a number of reasons. Aside from the Maine case, few activists are interested in buying inputs or selling food. The Maine case is also anomalous in that the model Local Food and Community Self-Governance Ordinance enacted in several townships uses a form of governance (not the absence of it) to protect small-scale producers. The approach of food sovereignty that favors the absence of governance also fails to understand how neoliberalism perpetuates the kinds of inequality that drove food sovereignty to emerge in the first place. It also fails to appreciate that we have not and never will buy and sell our way out of a crisis.

Another narrative of food sovereignty is national food self-sufficiency or state control over trade. This is usually articulated by activists who work against the WTO, such as Vandana Shiva. She and others articulate a strident political stance against supranational governing bodies that, in their view, frame policy to benefit transnational capital. They appeal to the state for protectionist trade policies and the stimulation of domestic production and distribution through the expansion of peasant rights, for example, through land reform. These narratives also resonate with the framing of political autonomy in the Nyéléni documents, but they do not address the underlying issue of liberal sovereignty and the way it enables capital accumulation, primarily in private sectors. None of the cases of food sovereignty activism that I investigated for this book articulated any faith in state governance as an enabler of food security. The White Earth example was the only case that demonstrated a need for governance by a "nation"—in this case the White Earth Tribe as an autonomous entity desiring overlapping sovereignties over shared territories. This is probably not what "national food self-sufficiency" advocates have in mind.

What I saw and heard most frequently in my research was an articulation of goals for radically collective notions of self-governance, egalitarian socionatural relationships, and the sharing of food through relations of care. The activists with whom I worked actively strove to achieve the social transformation and political autonomy that are prerequisite to those goals. They were not interested in getting the state off their backs so that they could sell more food and make more money. They also were not interested in asking the state for more protection. They sought to create the conditions of their own liberation through powerful articulations of connection both between people and with food and the natural world that makes food production possible. They were interested in producing more food for more people so that they could share it freely, barter, or in some cases sell it to members of the community in ways that sustainably provided for a food economy. They also worked to change the system from within. For example, the Athens permaculturalists understood they were working within a market system and focused on changing values by establishing connections that undermined the neoliberal mode of relating transactionally.

The problem in the food system, as food sovereignty activists profiled in this book see it, is not markets nor the role of governance but rather the way in which the territorial monopoly on coercive force is used to further the accumulation of capital in the corporate sector. This in itself is troubling, but over and over food sovereigntists have demonstrated that previously legal activities (gardening, selling raw milk, ricing, seed banking) have suddenly, nearly overnight, been deemed illegal and reframed as dangerous. This signals a definitional and political shift meant to terrorize people and make autonomous food production "unthinkable." The criminalization of food-producing activities occurs not because the saving of seed or the harvesting of rice poses some kind of real market threat to the food system or some kind of food safety risk but because activism is increasingly undermining the monopoly over ways of knowing food production that corporations enjoy. Knowledge is power, and in the case of food, knowledge is everything when it comes to producing and consuming.

Because of the friction of distance between producers and consumers in modernist agriculture as well as obfuscating tactics by corporations (e.g., anti-labeling laws, gag orders) consumers are alienated from the knowledge of food production. Some argue that if consumers "only knew" what goes on in the food system, they would make different choices, but consumers rarely make other choices about food purchasing decisions based on knowledge alone. This pervasive idea—that knowledge will change consumer behavior—drives many corporate efforts to perpetuate consumer alienation. Activists who want to educate eaters to make better choices—read: organic or Fair Trade—are distracted from the way in which income inequality drives choices more than knowledge does, and ultimately they play into the hand of corporate interests. Food sovereignty calls into question the justice of buying and selling food, as well as the way in which capitalism produces inequality such that consumers have few choices but to purchase the food that is produced through rationalized capitalist systems. Food sovereignty refocuses attention on the production of inequality and injustice and poses radical solutions through collective relations based on care.

Collapsing Binaries

Another significant and unexpected dimension of work for food sovereignty that I discovered in researching this book was the way in which activists operate between and across the binaries that shape the modernist food system. Capital-intensive agriculture discursively separates four realms of social life: political, economic, environmental, and cultural. The economic is separated from the political in modernist agriculture as narratives of free markets shape the production of commodities and belie the way in which subsidies and other public policies benefit corporations. The buying and selling of food separates food from its cultural significance in connecting people through sharing, reciprocity, and spirituality. The ecological is separated from everything else through the use of chemical inputs and a technological way of knowing the environment. Food sovereignty works to collapse these binaries to create new modes of production, new ways of relating, new ways of exchanging, and new ways of governing our food system that are deeply rooted in "old" ways of doing things.

Food sovereignty refocuses attention on unequal playing fields and how the economic must necessarily be political. Capital-intensive agriculture relies on state support to perpetuate itself but flies the flag of free markets. This has the effect of subordinating individual farmers, leading them to believe and engage in a competitive, zero-sum game with each other while corporations laugh all the way to the bank and farmers end up bankrupt. Food sovereignty exposes the lie of free markets and advocates for different forms of governance, with activists being willing to break the law if they have to in order to resist the problems of the modernist food system. Food sovereignty narratives call for political autonomy so that they can engage in acts of subsidiarity, or exchanges that do not require oversight by anyone but the two parties involved in the transaction. That subsidiarity is not allowed, even in the noncommercial exchange of seed, reveals the deceit of legislation that works under the guise of protecting consumers from unscrupulous businesspeople. To many food sovereigntists, the answer in this situation is not less government regulation but (1) exemption from regulation for mutual noncommercial exchanges; (2) rights to self-governance of exchange at a community scale when appropriate; (3) legislation that supports the general right and will of eaters and producers to self-govern territories and communities; and (4) exemption from costly inspections and processing requirements that are ill-suited to small-scale agricultural production.

Food sovereignty reconnects the natural and the cultural through agroecology. Agroecology, broadly defined, is an agricultural production model that presumes that the ecological processes and resources on which agriculture is based should be protected and nurtured. Organic agriculture is one form of agroecology, as are innumerable traditional practices, such as twelve-crop polyculture, which is widely practiced on Indian farms (Trauger, 2015). Permaculture is a particular form of agroecology that aims to mimic the natural systems in which food-bearing crops grow. Across a spectrum of modifications of the natural environment, permaculture might be seen as the least invasive and most ecologically beneficial of all cropping systems. It also has the potential to provide the highest yields of food crops per acre if citizen-eaters would be willing and able to (1) integrate food crops, such as blueberries, into landscaping; (2) integrate the growing and eating of permaculture crops into a daily pattern of life; and (3) create public spaces in which food can be grown for anyone to consume. Tree nut crops and backyard gardening are still widely practiced in Europe and the rest of the developing world. As demonstrated by the Athens case, this is a cultural shift that requires political will for the space to flourish, supported by the right to self-govern and the kinds of activism I've outlined in the preceding chapters.

Food sovereignty reconnects the cultural to the political and economic by reasserting a cultural value for food that supersedes its economic value as a commodity. The power of food is not in its capacity to generate profit through exchange but rather in its potential to generate connection through sharing and reciprocity. Food also has symbolic power, as demonstrated in the White Earth case; food security is the means and the end toward facilitating a deeper engagement with the self, the other, the natural, and the divine. When food is reduced to its value in an economic transaction, the spiritual and cultural power to reconnect people is stripped out of it. No doubt this is part of the project to alienate people from the means of production and from each other. Nothing brings people together quite like food, and nothing is more likely to be offered in times of crisis and need. The cultural power of food to forge connections and foment resistance should not be underestimated. As the White Earth case demonstrates, food has the power not only to provide for a community but also to feed resistance and fuel resilience through long periods of persecution.

Food sovereignty asks us to consider that we need to live within our ecological means and to not take more from the environment than it can support. This means, first and foremost, that we produce for subsistence, not for profit. If we follow that logical conclusion to its end, then food will lose its exchange value and be returned to having a use value, or an exchange value based on its use. If food and food production are returned to a primarily cultural, rather than economic, place in daily life, the use value of food (and of land, through the commons) can be reclaimed, and the tendency to reduce it to its exchange value can be resisted. People are hungry because they cannot afford to buy food, not because there is not enough food in the world. The simple truth of this is ignored and evaded by food security advocates who want to stimulate production and practice trickle-down economics, which we know will not work. Producing food in the place where it is consumed and making it free through community-based efforts stand a greater chance of addressing food security than any large-scale commodity program. This might sound ridiculous, but commodity-based programs continue to fail to feed people. It's time to try something different. Food sovereignty offers the world this possibility.

Taking It Home

The four case studies in this book reveal a number of insights about food sovereignty that are instructive for both scholars and activists. The first and probably most important is that resistance to liberal sovereignty is not futile, but it is criminalized or defined as dangerous and dumb. Resistance requires the implementation of specific spatial strategies to create zones of autonomy in which it can be practiced, in this case the production of food that the state and capital deem threatening to the neoliberal order. These spaces are often hidden or work through the margins—such as community gardens planted on properties that are hidden, public, or just not very valuable. Activists engaging in acts of civil disobedience, however, should be reminded that the liberal state holds the power of exception and advances the interests of capital, particularly in the United States, where governing commerce trumps all other rights.

Digesting this truth means that the demands for political autonomy sought by food sovereignty advocates, in both narrative and action, require a different kind of democracy. Figueroa (2013) defines this as a "people-centered" politics, which creates a space for the kinds of collective rights that the Nyéléni delegates say we need for food security. The Nyéléni documents are clear about how democracy needs to be done to achieve food security. They demand (1) state limits on corporations and on actions that give primacy to transnational trade over the food security needs of populations; (2) space for subsidiarity, especially in contexts in which people are already exchanging food in direct markets, such as the sale of raw milk or the exchange of seeds; (3) the development of regulations with broad notions of health in mind, rather than the development of narrowly defined food safety policies that primarily benefit large-scale producers and processors or require the purchase of costly equipment. Meeting these demands requires a politics of knowing that acknowledges the expertise of small-scale and technologically unsophisticated ways of food processing (i.e., on-farm chicken processing, raw milk) and recognizes that such processes might be superior to capital-intensive agricultural practices.

Alternative food networks have certainly done important work in advancing the popularity and availability of products such as farm-processed chicken and raw milk, but they also perpetuate market-based social relations and open up space for state-based regulation through their widening market share. There is nothing inherently wrong with exchange, whether it is for money or goods; the problem, however, arises through the way markets, with the support of the state, produce and perpetuate inequality, particularly in terms of access to food. Food sovereignty calls attention to the way in which state capitalism produces inequality, as well as why food is for sale in the first place and why it costs what it does, such that only some have access to food. It also demonstrates that food may, arguably, be produced in ways that benefit people, animals, and ecology. The Maine food sovereigntists, for example, were provoked through the implementation of legislation that required them to use but limited their access to USDA-inspected chicken-processing facilities. Being forced into such a model when there was no evidence that food sovereigntists' practices harmed anyone was an exercise of naked state power to legislate small-scale farmers out of existence and make alternative production models even more prohibitively expensive.

In the Maine case, food sovereignty represents the rights of farmers and eaters to produce and access a product that attempts to meet the social, economic, and environmental goals of sustainable agriculture. In so doing, it raises questions about the value of labor in large-scale slaughterhouses, where workers are not paid enough to purchase anything but mass-produced food. It also raises the issue of how the exchange value of the product is determined through the lack of state support for small-scale production and processing and clearly articulated state support for mass-produced chickens. In Georgia, the seventh-largest producer of broilers *in the world*, there are no USDA-inspected facilities for processing chickens on a small-scale. Farmers have to drive to North Carolina with their birds, which makes them too expensive for anyone but the very rich or the very committed. The sale of raw milk for human consumption is also banned in Georgia, as is travel across state lines to purchase it in South Carolina, where it is *somehow* safe to drink. The hypocrisy of free markets that prop up the fragile edifice of liberal democracy is laid bare in such examples. At least in Georgia, we won't buy and sell our way out of this problem, *because legally, we cannot.*

From one perspective, food sovereignty might be producing obedient neoliberal subjects who take responsibility for their own health and welfare. As such, food sovereignty may be seen as part of the postpolitical in its resignation to the inevitability of the neoliberal order (Mackinnon & Derickson, 2013). Seen another way, the resignation to neoliberalism may constitute a form of denial of the power of the (neo)liberal state through the design of systems, such as permaculture, that make it irrelevant (Ray, 2012). Resistance to the (neo)liberal state not only challenges it but also coproduces its existence by legitimating it. The production of alternative imaginaries of collective belonging to spaces and places outside of the state-capital nexus may already be creating radical alternative futures that make it irrelevant. These possibilities appear not without consequence on the political map, and as such, food sovereignty, with its attention to direct action, collective rights, and alternative democratic forms, deserves attention as a powerful alternative and corrective to the current neoliberal order.

Because food sovereignty does not yet seem able to resolve the tension between making claims on the state for rights and resisting the state's priorities, perhaps it requires a different kind of state. Perhaps the struggle to realize new rights and territorialize spaces in new ways is the process of creating a new state. This sovereign state would protect collective rights to access land (commons) and also collective rights to consume food, and not just the food that has been deemed "safe" by the powers that be. Speaking of situations in which individual and collective rights are in tension, Patel (2009) comes down in support of individual rights when put to the test, but he is speaking of a particular kind of contest: the rights of individual women over the collective rights of a community to enslave them. But in most areas of political action, individual and collective rights are not in conflict with each other. The right to bodily integrity and to collective access to land do not compete in a zero-sum game with each other, and if they did, individual rights could be granted *in addition to* collective rights. As Darrell of CELDF says, these are simply "rights that have not been enumerated yet." The state is a living thing that evolves with and through the participation of people who create rights, which we all participate in granting to each other. Similarly, sovereignty does not have to be a singularity. There can be sovereignties within sovereignties (Simpson, 2014), with power scaled down to individuals and communities when it comes to food production and exchange. The only reason that the current system does not do so is because of the way in which power is concentrated via corporate capital. Power should be dispersed and shared between individuals who belong to (in Gail Darrell's words, "are citizens of") their communities, which is exactly the kind of democracy that food sovereignty is asking us to think about.

While there are many other things that our new food sovereign state could or should do, I argue that the first order of business should be a new (not genocidal) Homestead Act. Several nonprofits accept donated land and provide it to aspiring farmers, who are mostly white and already privileged. This kind of ad-hoc land reform needs to be transformed into a more systematic redistribution, led by local governments and communities. The average age of farmers everywhere in the developed world is creeping up toward sixty. Their land does not need to be and should not be turned into the next parking lot to grow corn for ethanol. Their land needs to be given back to the people from whom it was stolen and returned to producing food that is native to that place. People with rights to land through this alternative distribution model would be Native Americans, then African Americans, first-generation migrants, and refugees from places the United States has destroyed with its foreign policies and wars. Finally, people of migrant settler descent should be given access. The only requirement for keeping the land should be to keep it in organic (not certified) production of native crops, sold through state-supported local and regional markets. Incentives to keep land communal will encourage cooperation. The priorities to protect seed, water, and soil that food sovereignty demands will follow from the work of thousands of new farmers tasked with protecting such priorities because they claim them, they share them, and they (and we) can't live without them.

Paying It Forward

So what does an advocate or activist for food sovereignty do? I suggest a few simple things, based on what I've learned from my activist research. The first is to advocate for commonsense legislation or amendments to current legislation around food production, distribution, and seed banking that benefit smallhold farmers and citizen-eaters. The USDA has comment periods that are supposedly an opportunity for the public to weigh in. Write letters, comment, use social networks to raise awareness. Advocate for Native American treaty rights wherever they are in dispute, and even when they aren't. Advocate for communal, collective land rights that include provisions for usufruct rights. This effort must be undertaken, as the alternative is to accept that the liberal democracy in which we live does not work. If you accept that the liberal state is hopelessly corrupt, then the work must be done through disobedience or through local-scale governance. Work to elect food sovereignty–friendly representatives to city councils, township boards, and state legislatures. Develop effective food sovereignty ordinances and advocate for them until they pass at a local scale. Develop a direct democracy party. Plant gardens and work to change the ordinances that ban them. Guerrilla garden. Buy raw milk and drink it. Keep backyard chickens. Plant a tree for freedom, or just a blueberry bush in the front yard. Resist enclosure. Resist waged work. Resist consumption. Grow, cook, and eat together.

While these efforts may seem idealistic, we work where we can and the process is the work. At a panel I convened on food sovereignty at the 2014 meeting of the Southeast Association of American Geographers, University of Georgia PhD student Richard Vercoe offered a lovely metaphor for thinking about food sovereignty in the context of neoliberalism. In response to a question from another University of Georgia PhD student, Gretchen Sneegas, about whether there is any reason to hope that food sovereignty could succeed, Vercoe offered the metaphor of seeds in the fruit of a plant. He said that a plant designed a fruit whose seeds could withstand the experience of digestion, given that the fruit entices an animal to eat the entire package, with the outcome being seed dispersal at the other end of the metabolic process. After painting a rather graphic and humorous picture, he said that we have to design food sovereignty in the same vein. Food sovereignty has to be able to withstand consumption and digestion as it passes through the body of the liberal sovereign state. How to do this is up to the activists who design, protect, and plant regenerative and self-replicating seeds of autonomy in the food system, starting with values that cannot be commodified—kindness and love.

From the failures of the alternative food movements, we know that buying and selling are not successful for realizing reform. This is exemplified in the concluding scenes of the popular film *Food Inc.* The last several moments are filled with thinly veiled messages about consumer politics being the answer to the food system ills that the producers and experts outline in the body of the film. A series of well-known food system critics—Michael Pollan, Eric Schlosser, and other "big organic" executives—take up the closing montage, advocating for buying organic, buying Fair Trade, even shopping at big-box retailers that stock their shelves with organic products. In short, they believe that we can buy and sell our way out of inequality, hunger, and injustice. The gendered, raced, and classed myopia of this utopian vision is nearly indigestible. It misses so much. Fortunately food sovereignty refocuses our attention on the social, economic, and environmental issues that motivated organic farmers and Fair Trade and local food advocates in the first place. These problems haven't gone away in spite of the relative success of those niche markets.

In contrast, the concluding message at the end of *The Power of Community: How Cuba Survived Peak Oil* is simple and has nothing to do with buying and selling. The film details how Cuba experienced a catastrophic blow to its industrialized, petroleum- and import-dependent agriculture after the fall of the Soviet Union. During the so-called Special Period, which lasted five years, the average Cuban lost twenty pounds. Cuba is an interesting case study in food sovereignty, not only because of the way in which it had to reorganize food production to feed itself but also because it had to retool the way in which food was produced and where, and how it was distributed to a hungry population. One of the most powerful tools that Cuba used was the implementation of permaculture systems in community and home gardens on collective and privately held lands. A number of practitioners and advocates are interviewed throughout the film, and their explanations about why permaculture worked to feed Cuba's population resonate with the permaculturalists I interviewed across the United States and Europe and the anarchists who came before them. At the very end of the film, a Cuban agronomist concludes, "What we need is more friendship and *more love*. We only have one world. The world is one, and it's for all of us."

So, in a word, love.

APPENDIX

An Ordinance to Protect the Health and Integrity of the Local Food System in the Town of ____(Name Of Town)____ , ____(Name Of County)____ County, Maine.

Section 1. Name. This Ordinance shall be known and may be cited as the "Local Food and Community Self-Governance Ordinance."

Section 2. Definitions. As used in this ordinance:

(a) "Patron" means an individual who is the last person to purchase any product or preparation directly from a processor or producer and who does not resell the product or preparation.

(b) "Home consumption" means consumed within a private home.

(c) "Local Foods" means any food or food product that is grown, produced, or processed by individuals who sell directly to their patrons through farm-based sales or buying clubs, at farmers markets, roadside stands, fundraisers or at community social events.

(d) "Processor" means any individual who processes or prepares products of the soil or animals for food or drink.

(e) "Producer" means any farmer or gardener who grows any plant or animal for food or drink.

(f) "Community social event" means an event where people gather as part of a community for the benefit of those gathering, or for the community, including but not limited to a church or religious social, school event, potluck, neighborhood gathering, library meeting, traveling food sale, fundraiser, craft fair, farmers market and other public events.

Section 3. Preamble and Purpose. We the People of the Town of ____(name of town)____ , ____(name of county)____ County, Maine have the right to produce, process, sell, purchase and consume local foods thus promoting self-reliance, the preservation of family farms, and local food traditions. We recognize that family farms, sustainable agricultural practices, and food processing by individuals, families and non-corporate entities offers stability to our rural way of life by enhancing the economic, environmental and social wealth of our community. As such, our right to a local food system requires us to assert our inherent right to self-government. We recognize the authority to protect that right as belonging to the Town of ___(name of town)___ .

We have faith in our citizens' ability to educate themselves and make informed decisions. We hold that federal and state regulations impede local food production and constitute a usurpation of our citizens' right to foods of their choice. We support food that fundamentally respects human dignity and health, nourishes individuals and the community, and sustains producers, processors and the environment. We are therefore duty bound under the Constitution of the State of Maine to protect and promote unimpeded access to local foods.

The purpose of the Local Food and Community Self-Governance Ordinance is to:

(i)   Provide citizens with unimpeded access to local food;
(ii) Enhance the local economy by promoting the production and purchase of local agricultural products;
(iii) Protect access to farmers' markets, roadside stands, farm based sales and direct producer to patron sales;
(iv) Support the economic viability of local food producers and processors;
(v)   Preserve community social events where local foods are served or sold;
(vi) Preserve local knowledge and traditional foodways.

Section 4. Authority. This Ordinance is adopted and enacted pursuant to the inherent, inalienable, and fundamental right of the citizens of the Town of ___(name of town)___ to self-government, and under the authority recognized as belonging to the people of the Town by all relevant state and federal laws including, but not limited to the following:

The Declaration of Independence of the United States of America, which declares that governments are instituted to secure peoples' rights, and that government derives its just powers from the consent of the governed.
Article I, § 2 of the Maine Constitution, which declares: "all power is inherent in the people; all free governments are founded in their authority and instituted for their benefit, [and that] they have therefore an unalienable and indefensible right to institute government and to alter, reform, or totally change the same when their safety and happiness require it."
§3001 of Title 30–A of the Maine Revised Statutes, which grants municipalities all powers necessary to protect the health, safety, and welfare of the residents of the Town of ___(name of town)___ .
§211 of Title 7 of the Maine Revised Statutes which states: "it is the policy of the State to encourage food self-sufficiency for the State."

Section 5. Statements of Law.

Section 5.1. Licensure/Inspection Exemption. Producers or processors of local foods in the Town of _____(name of town)_____ are exempt from licensure and inspection provided that the transaction is only between the producer or processor and a patron when the food is sold for home consumption. This includes any producer or processor who sells his or her products at farmers' markets or roadside stands; sells his or her products through farm-based sales directly to a patron; or delivers his or her products directly to patrons.

Section 5.1.a. Licensure/Inspection Exemption. Producers or processors of local foods in the Town of _____(name of town)_____ are exempt from licensure and inspection provided that their products are prepared for, consumed, or sold at a community social event.

Section 5.2. Right to Access and Produce Food. _____(name of town)_____ citizens possess the right to produce, process, sell, purchase, and consume local foods of their choosing.

Section 5.3. Right to Self-Governance. All citizens of _____(name of town)_____ possess the right to a form of governance which recognizes that all power is inherent in the people, that all free governments are founded on the people's authority and consent.

Section 5.4. Right to Enforce. _____(name of town)_____ citizens possess the right to adopt measures which prevent the violation of the rights enumerated in this Ordinance.

Section 6. Statement of Law. Implementation. The following restrictions and provisions serve to implement the preceding statements of law.

Section 6.1. State and Federal Law. It shall be unlawful for any law or regulation adopted by the state or federal government to interfere with the rights recognized by this Ordinance. It shall be unlawful for any corporation to interfere with the rights recognized by this Ordinance. The term "corporation" shall mean any business entity organized under the laws of any state or country.

Section 6.2. Patron Liability Protection. Patrons purchasing food for home consumption may enter into private agreements with those producers or processors of local foods to waive any liability for the consumption of that food. Producers or processors of local foods shall be exempt from licensure and inspection requirements for that food as long as those agreements are in effect.

Section 7. Civil Enforcement. The Town of _____(name of town)_____ may enforce the provisions of this Ordinance through seeking equitable relief from a court of competent jurisdiction. Any individual citizen of the Town of _____(name of town)___ shall have standing to vindicate any rights secured by this ordinance which have been violated or which are threatened with violation, and may seek relief both in the form of injunctive and compensatory relief from a court of competent jurisdiction.

Section 8. Town Action against Pre-emption. The foundation for making and adoption of this law is the peoples' fundamental and inalienable right to govern themselves, and thereby secure their rights to life, liberty, and the pursuit of happiness. Any attempt to use other units and levels of government to preempt, amend, alter or overturn this Ordinance or parts of this Ordinance shall require the Town to hold public meetings that explore the adoption of other measures that expand local control and the ability of citizens to protect their fundamental and inalienable right to self-government. It is declared that those other measures may legitimately include the partial or complete separation of the Town from the other units and levels of government that attempt to preempt, amend, alter, or overturn this Ordinance.

Section 9. Effect. This Ordinance shall be effective immediately upon its enactment.

Section 10. Severability Clause. To the extent any provision of this Ordinance is deemed invalid by a court of competent jurisdiction, such provision will be removed from the Ordinance, and the balance of the Ordinance shall remain valid.

Section 11. Repealer. All inconsistent provisions of prior Ordinances adopted by the Town of ___(name of town)___ are hereby repealed, but only to the extent necessary to remedy the inconsistency.

NOTES

Introduction. Political Practice at the Margins

1. In this text, food sovereignty practices include, but are not limited to, community-based agriculture on squatted land, community food centers, seed-saving collectives, noncommodified food exchanges, or food production, consumption, and distribution practices that fall outside the corporate food regime, which includes "big organic" and Fair Trade.

2. I developed this framework in collaboration with an MA student, Molly Canfield, who completed a thesis on urban livestock titled "Backyards as Borderlands" under my supervision at the University of Georgia in 2014.

3. Marc Edelman (2014) asserts that *food sovereignty* first emerged as a term in the Mexican PRONAL, the national food policy under the PRI in 1983.

4. I rely on the Nyéléni Declaration for the majority of my analysis in this book because it overtly emphasizes the role of political sovereignty in relation to land, economy, society, and food production models.

5. The word *radical* is used throughout this book to indicate systemic change that often requires dismantling existing social, economic, and political arrangements, in much the same way that "radical feminism" advances its agenda for change.

6. However short-lived this experiment was, however, thirty years later I still sleep under a quilt made from the raw wool of those sheep.

7. In mid-2014 I rehomed my two chickens to a farm that I visit frequently. This action was provoked by a dispute with my neighbor over the chemical trespass of 2, 4–D on my food plants in the front yard. My chickens were reported to the authorities shortly after I asked my neighbor to stop spraying my plants. I moved them to be on the right side of a dispute with my neighbors, who apparently don't want them nearby, rather than because of the law. In this case, the complaint arose over my unwillingness to be poisoned.

8. In my case it was likely exposure to residues of dioxin-contaminated Agent Orange, which was sprayed in the headwaters region of Minnesota until 1970.

Chapter 1. Political Economies of Food Sovereignty

1. This big-tent vision, however, contains some potentially damning contradictions. Patel (2009), Agarwal (2014), and others have elaborated at length on these contradic-

tions, such as the tension between individual and collective rights and tensions between national and local food self-sufficiency.

2. The seven themes are: (1) local markets and international trade policies, (2) local knowledge and technology, (3) access to and control over natural resources, (4) sharing territories and land, (5) conflicts and natural disasters, (6) social conditions and forced migration, and (7) production models.

3. Throughout the remainder of the book, I refer to this mutual co-constitution of capital and geopolitical power in the sovereignty of the national state with the terms *state/capital* and *(neo)liberal states*. *State/capital* refers to the way capital works in and through the state regulatory apparatus and the way state power capitalizes on free market ideology. *(Neo)liberal states* refers to entities in which neoliberalism is embedded and arises from liberal democratic rights.

4. State overthrow has never been, nor will it ever be, the answer to securing food for populations.

Chapter 2. Episteme(s) of Food Sovereignty

1. This quote is often attributed to Paul Wellstone, the late senator from Minnesota.

Chapter 3. Temporary Commons

1. Unless both first and last names are used, all names given in case studies are pseudonyms.

2. Ollas irrigation systems use unglazed clay pots to capture and store water underground.

Chapter 4. Spatial Practices of Governance

1. Paradoxically, the rapid increase in the adoption of organic agriculture has ultimately led to the reintensification of environmentally unfriendly practices (Trauger & Murphy, 2013).

2. The FDA responded favorably to a substantial amount of outrage and impassioned advocacy by small-scale farmers and their defenders and extended the comment period for the act. The new rules are set to be officially registered as of June 30, 2015.

Chapter 5. Re/territorializing Food Security

1. All population figures are from the 2000 Census. Information is taken from U.S. Census Bureau, "QuickFacts," https://www.census.gov/quickfacts/table/PST045215/00.

2. The route planned in 2014 for an Enbridge oil pipeline through the watersheds of northern Minnesota has met fierce resistance from the tribes living there for this reason.

Chapter 6. Making Political Space for Life

1. See references to recent federal cases against raw milk producers and food-buying clubs in the film *Farmageddon* (Canty, 2011).

2. There is a long history of the revolving door between corporations and government officials. Henry A. Wallace, secretary of agriculture under FDR, was the former president of Pioneer Hi-Bred seed company and authorized the expenditure of public funds on research into plant genetics in 1935.

3. Vandana Shiva's research farm in India, at which I stayed for two months, has a house dedicated to Fukoaka, which was directly across from my room at the farm.

4. Athens Locally Grown, the software used by this online farmers market, was developed by a programmer in Athens and has since spread nationally. The open-source software is free to use, although a small royalty is generated on total sales of goods sold using the software.

REFERENCES

Agamben, G. (2005). *State of exception*. Chicago: University of Chicago Press.

Agarwal, B. (2014). Food sovereignty, food security and democratic choice: Critical contradictions and difficult conciliations. *Journal of Peasant Studies, 41*(6), 1247–1268.

Agnew, J. (2005). Sovereignty regimes: Territoriality and state authority in contemporary world politics. *Annals of the Association of American Geographers, 95*(2), 437–461.

Agnew, J. (2009). *Globalization and sovereignty*. Lanham, Md.: Rowman and Littlefield.

Alkon, A. H., and T. M. Mares. (2012). Food sovereignty in U.S. food movements: Radical visions and neoliberal constraints. *Agriculture and Human Values, 29*(3), 347–359.

Allen, P. (1999). Reweaving the food security safety net: Mediating entitlement and entrepreneurship. *Agriculture and Human Values, 16*(2), 117–129.

Allen, P. (2004). *Together at the table: Sustainability and sustenance in the American agrifood system*. State College: Pennsylvania State University Press.

Allen, P., and M. Kovach. (2000). The capitalist composition of organic: The potential of markets in fulfilling the promise of organic agriculture. *Agriculture and Human Values, 17*(3), 221–232.

Almy R. (2013). *State v. Brown*: A test for local food ordinances. *Maine Law Review, 65*(2), 790–805.

Altieri, M., and C. Nicholls. (2008). Scaling up agroecological approaches for food sovereignty in Latin America. *Development, 51*(4), 472–480.

Alvarez, Sonia E., Evelina Dagnino, and Arturo Escobar (Eds.). (1998). *Culture of politics—politics of culture: Re-visioning Latin American social movements*. Boulder, Colo.: Westview Press.

Anderson, J. (1996). The shifting state of politics: New medieval and postmodern territorialities? *Environment and Planning D: Society and Space, 14*, 133–153.

Anderson, M. D., and J. T. Cook. (1999). Community food security: Practice in need of theory?. *Agriculture and Human Values, 16*(2), 141–150.

Aoki, K. (2003). Weeds, seeds and (and) deeds: Recent skirmishes in the seed wars. *Cardozo Journal of International and Comparative Law, 11*, 247.

Appadurai, A. (Ed.). (1988). *The social life of things: Commodities in cultural perspective.* New York: Cambridge University Press.

Appadurai, A. (1996). *Modernity at large: Cultural dimensions of globalization.* Public Worlds, vol. 1. Minneapolis: University of Minnesota Press.

Appadurai, A. (2003). Sovereignty without territoriality: Notes for a postnational geography. In P. Yaeger (Ed.), *The geography of identity* (pp. 40–58). Ann Arbor: University of Michigan Press.

Appadurai, A. (2006). The thing itself. *Public Culture, 18*(1), 15.

ASTA. (2014). American Seed Trade Association. Retrieved April 10, 2015, from http:// www.amseed.org/.

Araujo, M. (2013). After two decade occupation, MST families win land rights. Retrieved March 26, 2015, from http://www.grassrootsonline.org/news/blog/after -two-decade-occupation-mst-families-win-land-rights.

Bangor Daily News. (2011). State sues Blue Hill farmer for selling unpasteurized milk at farmers' markets. Retrieved February 12, 2012, from http://bangordailynews.com /2011/11/16/news/hancock/blue-hill-farmer-cited-for-violating-state-law/.

Bangor Daily News. (2014). Blue Hill's Farmer Brown loses three year fight against dairy regulation. Retrieved June 13, 2015, from http://bangordailynews.com/2014 /06/17/politics/blue-hills-farmer-brown-loses-three-year-fight-against-state-dairy -regulation/.

Barkan, J. (2013). *Corporate sovereignty.* Minneapolis: University of Minnesota Press.

Barrett, C. B. (2002). Food security and food assistance programs. *Handbook of agricultural economics, 2,* 2103–2190.

Barry, B. (1999). Sustainability and intergenerational justice. In A. Dobson (Ed.), *Fairness and futurity: Essays on sustainability and social justice* (pp. 93–117). Oxford: Oxford University Press.

Bates, A., and T. Hemenway. (2010). From agriculture to permaculture. In Linda Starke and Lisa Mastny (eds.), *State of the world 2010: Transforming cultures from consumerism to sustainability: A Worldwatch Institute report on progress toward a sustainable society* (pp. 47–53). New York: W. W. Norton.

Bee, B., J. Rice, and A. Trauger. (2015). A feminist approach to climate change governance: Everyday and intimate politics. *Geography Compass, 9,* 339–350.

Bello, W. (2009). *The food wars.* Verso: London.

Benhabib, S. (2004). *The rights of others: Aliens, residents, and citizens.* Cambridge, Mass.: Cambridge University Press.

Berleant, A. (2013, September 12). Department of Agriculture cites Dan Brown for pesticide purchase. *Weekly Packet.* Retrieved March 5, 2015, from https:// penobscotbaypress.com/news/2013/sep/12/department-of-agriculture-cites-dan -brown-for-2010/#.VPe5R_nF-So.

Bey, H. (2003). *The temporary autonomous zone: Ontological anarchy, poetic terrorism* (2nd ed.). New York: Autonomedia.

Bishop, P., and L. Williams. (2012). *The temporary city.* London: Routledge.

Blakeney, M. (2011). Recent developments in intellectual property and power in the private sector related to food and agriculture. *Food Policy, 36,* s109–s113.

Borras, S., Jr. and J. Franco. (2012). *A "land sovereignty" alternative? Towards a peoples' counter-enclosure.* Amsterdam: Transnational Institute.

Boulanger, P. M. (2010). Three strategies for sustainable consumption. *S.A.P.I.E.N.S.: Surveys and Perspectives Integrating Environment and Society, 3*(2).

Bower, R. W., Jr. (1985). Home rule and the pre-emption doctrine: The relationship between state and local government in Maine. *Maine Law Review, 37,* 313–365.

Breitbart, M. (1978). Anarchist decentralism in rural Spain, 1936–1939: The integration of community and environment. *Antipode, 10*(3-1), 83–98.

Brenner, N. (1999). Beyond state-centricism? Space, territoriality, and geographical scale in globalization studies. *Theory and Society, 28,* 39–78.

Brenni, C. (2015). Where are the local communities? Food sovereignty discourse on international agrobiodiversity conservation strategies. In A. Trauger (Ed.), *Food sovereignty in international context: Discourse, politics and practice of place* (pp. 15–34). New York: Routledge.

Buck, D., C. Getz, and J. Guthman. (1997). From farm to table: The organic vegetable commodity chain of Northern California. *Sociologia Ruralis, 37*(1), 3–20.

Burawoy, M. (Ed.) (2000). *Global ethnography: Forces, connections, and imaginations in a postmodern world.* Berkeley: University of California Press.

Burke, B. J. (2012). *"Para que cambiemos"/"So we can (ex) change": Economic activism and socio-cultural change in the barter systems of Medellín, Colombia.* Unpublished PhD thesis. University of Arizona.

Cadman, L. (2010). "How (not) to be governed: Foucault, critique, and the political." *Environment and Planning D: Society and Space, 28*(3), 539–556.

Canfield, M. (2014). *Backyards as borderlands: Humans, animals and urban food production.* Unpublished MA thesis. University of Georgia.

Canty, Kristin (Director). (2011). *Farmageddon.* Metuchen, N.J.: Passion River Films.

Carson, K. A. (2007). *Studies in mutualist political economy.* N.p.: Book Surge.

Carlsson, C., and F. Manning. (2010). Nowtopia: Strategic exodus? *Antipode, 42*(4), 924–953.

CELDF (Community Environmental Legal Defense Fund). (2015). Retrieved June 3, 2015, from celdf.org.

Charvet, J., and E. Kaczynska-Nay. (2008). *The liberal project and human rights: The theory and practice of a new world order.* Cambridge: Cambridge University Press.

Chou, J. (2010). *Insurgent public space: Guerrilla urbanism and the remaking of contemporary cities.* London: Routledge.

Claeys, P. (2012). The creation of new rights by the food sovereignty movement: The challenge of institutionalizing subversion. *Sociology, 46*(5), 844–860.

Clapp, J. (2012). *Food.* Cambridge: Polity Press.

Clinton v. Cedar Rapids and the Missouri River Railroad, 24 Iowa 455 (1868).

Clough, N., and R. Blumberg. (2012). Toward anarchist and autonomist Marxist geographies. *ACME: An International E-Journal for Critical Geographies, 11,* 335–351.

Coleman, M. (2009). What counts as the politics and practice of security, and where? Devolution and immigrant insecurity after 9/11. *Annals of the Association of American Geographers, 99*(5), 904–913.

Creason, Naomi. (2014a, July 31). Department of Agriculture cracks down on seed libraries. *Carlisle (Penn.) Sentinel.* Retrieved April 10, 2015, from http://cumberlink .com/news/local/communities/carlisle/department-of-agriculture-cracks-down -on-seed-libraries/article_8b0323f4-18f6-11e4-b4c1-0019bb2963f4.html.

Creason, Naomi. (2014b, August 5). PA department backs seed library protocol as reaction grows. *Carlisle (Penn.) Sentinel*. Retrieved April 10, 2015, from http://cumberlink.com/news/agriculture/pa-department-backs-seed-library-protocol-as-reaction-grows/article_d3acf6fc-1cf2-11e4-adf9-0019bb2963f4.html.

Curry, G. N. (2003). Moving beyond postdevelopment: Facilitating indigenous alternatives for "development." *Economic Geography, 79*(4), 405–423.

Dawson, A. (2010). Introduction: New enclosures. *New Formations, 69*(1), 8–22.

DeLind, L. B. (2002). Place, work, and civic agriculture: Common fields for cultivation. *Agriculture and Human Values, 19*(3), 217–224.

Deleuze, G., and F. Guattari. (1987). *A thousand plateaus*. (B. Massumi, Trans.). Minneapolis: University of Minnesota Press.

Desmarais, A. A. (2007). *La vía campesina: Globalization and the power of peasants*. Halifax, N.S.: Fernwood Publishing and Pluto Press.

Desmarais, A. A. (2012). *La vía campesina*. New York: John Wiley and Sons.

Desmarais, A. A., and H. Wittman. (2014). "Farmers, foodies and first nations: Getting to food sovereignty in Canada." *Journal of Peasant Studies, 41*(6), 1153–1173.

DBCFSN (Detroit Black Farmers Food Security Network). (2015). Retrieved April 10, 2015, from http://detroitblackfoodsecurity.org/index.html.

Diller, P. A. (2007). Intrastate preemption. *Boston University Law Review, 87*(5), 1113–76.

Dillon, M. (2005, March/April). Monsanto buys Seminis. *Organic Broadcaster*. Retrieved March 4, 2015, from http://newfarm.rodaleinstitute.org/features/2005/0205/seminisbuy.

Donald, B., and Blay-Palmer, A. (2006). The urban creative-food economy: Producing food for the urban elite or social inclusion opportunity? *Environment and Planning A, 38*(10), 1901.

Dunn, E. C. (2003). Trojan pig: Paradoxes of food safety regulation. *Environment and Planning A, 35*(8), 1493–1511.

DuPuis, E. M., and D. Goodman, D. (2005). Should we go "home" to eat?: Toward a reflexive politics of localism. *Journal of Rural Studies, 21*(3), 359–371.

Edelman, M. (2014). Food sovereignty: Forgotten genealogies and future regulatory challenges. *Journal of Peasant Studies, 41*(6), 959–978.

Elden, S. (2010). Land, terrain, territory. *Progress in Human Geography 34*(6), 799–817.

Fairbairn, M. (2010). Framing resistance: International food regimes and the roots of food sovereignty. In H. Wittman, A. A. Desmarais, and N. Wiebe (Eds.), *Food sovereignty: Reconnecting food, nature and community*, (pp. 15–32). Halifax, N.S.: Fernwood Publishing.

Faubion, J. D. (1994). *Michel Foucault, power: The essential works of Foucault, 1954–1984*. Vol. 3 New York: New Press.

Feagan, R. (2007). The place of food: Mapping out the "local" in local food systems. *Progress in Human Geography, 31*(1), 23–42.

Feeding America (2011). *Hunger in America*. Retrieved April 10, 2015, from https://feedingamerica.org/hunger-in-america/hunger-studies/map-the-meal-gap/~/media/Files/a-map-2011/2011-mmg-exec-summary.ashx.

Figueroa, M. (2013). Food sovereignty in everyday life: A people-centered approach to food systems. Paper presented at Food Sovereignty: A Critical Dialogue, Yale University.

Foucault, M. (1978). "Part five: Right of death and power over life." In *The History of Sexuality* (Vol. 1) (pp. 135–159). New York: Vintage Books.

Foucault, M. (1991). "Governmentality." In M. Foucault, G. Burchell, C. Gordon, and P. Miller (Eds.), *The Foucault effect: Studies in governmentality* (pp. 87–104). Chicago: University of Chicago Press.

Foucault, M. (2002). *The order of things: An archaeology of the human sciences.* London: Psychology Press.

Foucault, M. (2003). *Society must be defended: Lectures at the College de France, 1975–76.* (M. Bertani and A. Fontana, Eds., A. Davidson, English series Ed., D. Macey, Trans.). New York: Picador.

Fowler, C. (1994). *Unnatural selection: Technology, politics, and plant evolution* (Vol. 6). Yverdon, Switzerland: Gordon and Breach.

Friedmann, H. (1980). Household production and the national economy: Concepts for the analysis of agrarian formations. *Journal of Peasant Studies, 7*(2), 158–184.

Friedmann, H. (1993, January–February). The political economy of food: A global crisis. *New Left Review, 197,* 29–57.

Friedmann, H., and P. McMichael, P. (1989). Agriculture and the state system: The rise and decline of national agricultures, 1870 to the present. *Sociologia ruralis, 29*(2), 93–117.

Fukuoka, M. (2009). *The one-straw revolution: An introduction to natural farming.* Emmaus, Penn.: Rodale Press.

Garland, C. (2010). The (anti-)politics of autonomy: Between Marxism and anarchism. *Theory in Action, 3*(4), 8–16.

Gibson-Graham, J. K. (1994). "Stuffed if I know!": Reflections on post-modern feminist social research. *Gender, Place and Culture: A Journal of Feminist Geography, 1*(2), 205–224.

Gibson-Graham, J. K. (2006). *A postcapitalist politics.* Minneapolis: University of Minnesota Press.

Gidwani, V. (2008). *Capital, interrupted: Agrarian development and the politics of work in India.* Minneapolis: University of Minnesota Press.

Gilbert, J., S. D. Wood, and G. Sharp. (2002). Who owns the land? Agricultural land ownership by race/ethnicity. *Rural America, 17*(4), 55–62.

Gille, Z., and S. Ó. Riain. (2002). Global ethnography. *Annual Review of Sociology, 28*(1), 271–295.

Gilroy, P. (1993). *The black Atlantic: Modernity and double consciousness.* Cambridge, Mass.: Harvard University Press.

Goldman, E. (1972). *Red Emma speaks: Selected writings and speeches.* (Shulman, A. K., Ed.) New York: Vintage Books.

Goodman, D., and M. Redclift. (1991). *Refashioning nature: Food, ecology and culture.* London: Routledge.

Goodman, D., and Watts, M. (Eds.). (1997). *Globalising food: Agrarian questions and global restructuring.* London: Routledge.

Gordon, U. (2007). Anarchism reloaded. *Journal of Political Ideologies, 12*(1), 29–48.

Gottlieb, R., and A. Joshi. (2010). *Food justice.* Cambridge, Mass.: MIT Press.

Graeber, D. (2009). *Direct action: An ethnography.* Edinburgh: AK press.

Gregory, Chris. (1982). *Gifts and Commodities.* London: Academic Press.

Guthman, J. (1998). Regulating meaning, appropriating nature: The codification of California organic agriculture. *Antipode, 30*(2), 135–154.

Guthman, J. (2008a). Bringing good food to others: Investigating the subjects of alternative food practice. *Cultural Geographies, 15*(4), 431–447.

Guthman, J. (2008b). Neoliberalism and the making of food politics in California. *Geoforum, 39*(3), 1171–1183.

Guthman, J. (2011). *Weighing in: Obesity, food justice, and the limits of capitalism.* California Studies in Food and Culture, Vol. 32. Berkeley: University of California Press.

Habermas, J. (1987). *The philosophical discourse of modernity.* Cambridge: Polity Press.

Halper, E. (2014, February 22). Planned food safety rules rile organic farmers. *Los Angeles Times.* Retrieved February 28, 2014, from http://www.latimes.com/nation/la-na-food-safety-20140223,0,6831660.story?page=1#axzz2ueJr1ng2.

Haraway, D. (1988). Situated knowledges: The science question in feminism and the privilege of partial perspective. *Feminist Studies, 14*(3), 575–599.

Hardt, M., and A. Negri. (2004). *Multitude: War and democracy in the age of empire.* Penguin: New York.

Hardt, M., and A. Negri. (2009). *Empire.* Cambridge, Mass.: Harvard University Press.

Harrison, K. L. (2008). Organic plus: Regulating beyond the current organic standards. *Pace Environmental Law Review, 25*, 211.

Harriss, J. (Ed.). (1982). *Rural development: Theories of peasant economy and agrarian change.* London: Hutchinson University Library.

Harvey, D. (1990). *The condition of postmodernity: An enquiry into the conditions of cultural change.* Oxford: Blackwell.

Harvey, D. (2003). *The new imperialism.* Oxford: Oxford University Press.

Hawley, B. A. (1980). Treaty interpretation—off-reservation rights—Chippewa Indians retain no off-reservation right to harvest wild rice without Minnesota license. *Hamline Law Review, 4*, 373.

Hébert, K, and D. Mincyte. (2014). Self-reliance beyond neoliberalism: Rethinking autonomy at the edges of empire. *Environment and Planning D: Society and Space, 32*(2), 206–222.

Hemenway, T. (2009). *Gaia's garden: A guide to home-scale permaculture.* White River Junction, Vt.: Chelsea Green.

Henderson, G. (2004). "Free" food, the local production of worth, and the circuit of decommodification: A value theory of the surplus. *Environment and Planning D, 22*(4), 485–512.

Heynen, N., J. McCarthy, S. Prudham, and P. Robbins (Eds.). (2007). *Neoliberal environments: False promises and unnatural consequences.* New York: Routledge.

Hinrichs, C. C. (2000). Embeddedness and local food systems: Notes on two types of direct agricultural market. *Journal of Rural Studies, 16*(3), 295–303.

Holston, J. (1998). Spaces of insurgent citizenship. In L. Sandercock (Ed.), *Making the invisible visible: A multi-cultural planning history* (pp. 37–56). Berkeley: University of California Press.

Holt-Giménez, E., and L. Peabody. (2008). From food rebellions to food sovereignty: Urgent call to fix a broken food system. *Food First Backgrounder, 14*(1), 1–6.

Holt-Giménez, E., and A. Shattuck. (2011). Food crises, food regimes and food movements: Rumblings of reform or tides of transformation? *Journal of Peasant Studies, 38*(1), 109–144.

hooks, b. (2006). Love as the Practice of Freedom. In *Outlaw Culture: Resisting Representations* (pp. 289–298). New York: Routledge.

Horta do Monte. (n.d.) Long description [Facebook page]. Retrieved May 18, 2016, from www.facebook.com/hortadomonte/info.

Hospes, Otto. (2014). Food sovereignty: The debate, the deadlock, and a suggested detour. *Agriculture and Human Values, 31*(1), 119–130.

Illich, I., (1976). *Medical nemesis: The expropriation of health.* New York: Pantheon.

Ince, A. (2012). In the shell of the old: Anarchist geographies of territorialisation. *Antipode, 44*(5), 1645–1666.

Indian Fishing and Hunting Rights. (2014). *Minnesota Legislative Reference Library.* Retrieved August 29, 2014, from http://www.leg.state.mn.us/lrl/issues/issues.aspx ?issue=indian.

Jarosz, L. (2008). The city in the country: Growing alternative food networks in metropolitan areas. *Journal of Rural Studies, 24*(3), 231–244.

Jellison, K. (1993). *Entitled to power: Farm women and technology, 1913–1963.* Chapel Hill: University of North Carolina Press.

Kautsky, K. (1988). *The agrarian question.* (H. Alavi, Trans.). (Vol. 2). London: Zwan.

Kloppenburg, J. R. (2005). *First the seed: The political economy of plant biotechnology.* Madison: University of Wisconsin Press.

Kloppenburg, J. R. (2010). Impeding dispossession, enabling repossession: Biological open source and the recovery of seed sovereignty. *Journal of agrarian change, 10*(3), 367–388.

Koc, M., R. MacRae, L. J. A. Mougeot, and J. Walsh. (1999). *Hunger-proof cities: Sustainable urban food systems.* Ottawa: International Research Development Center.

Kropotkin, Petr. (1907). *The conquest of bread.* London: J. P. Putnam's Sons.

Kurtz, H. (2013). Scaling biopolitics: Enacting food sovereignty in Maine (USA). Paper presented at Food Sovereignty: A Critical Dialogue, Yale University. Retrieved November 18, 2013, from http://www.yale.edu/agrarianstudies/foodsovereignty/pprs /40_Kurtz_2013.pdf.

Kurtz, H., A. Trauger, and C. Passidomo. (2013). The contested terrain of biological citizenship in the seizure of raw milk in Athens, Georgia. *Geoforum, 48,* 136–144.

Lamborn, P., and B. Weinberg (Eds.). (1999). *Avant gardening: Ecological struggle in the city and the world.* New York: Autonomedia.

Landes, J. B. (1988). *Women and the public sphere: In the age of the French Revolution.* Ithaca, N.Y.: Cornell University Press.

Latour, B. (1993). *We have never been modern.* Cambridge, Mass.: Harvard University Press.

Latour, B. (2004). How to talk about the body? The normative dimension of science studies. *Body and society, 10*(2–3), 205–229.

Laugesen, M., and R. B. Elliott. (2003). Ischaemic heart disease, Type 1 diabetes, and cow milk A1 β-casein. *New Zealand Medical Journal, 116*(1168), 1–19.

LeCompte, M. D., and J. J. Schensul (Eds.). (1999). *Designing and conducting ethnographic research.* Walnut Creek, Calif.: Altamira.

Lefebvre, H. (1991). *The production of space.* (Donald Nicholson-Smith, Trans.). Oxford: Blackwell.

Levinsohn, J., and M. McMillan. (2007). Does food aid harm the poor? Household evidence from Ethiopia. In Ann E. Harrison (Ed.), *Globalization and Poverty* (pp. 561–598). Chicago: University of Chicago Press.

Levkoe, C. Z. (2006). Learning democracy through food justice movements. *Agriculture and Human Values, 23*(1), 89–98.

LVC. La Via Campesina. (2012). Retrieved June 5, 2012, from http://viacampesina.org/en/.

Lyson, T. A. (2004). *Civic agriculture: Reconnecting farm, food, and community.* Lebanon, N.H.: University Press of New England.

Lyson, T. A., and A. Guptill. (2004). Commodity agriculture, civic agriculture and the future of U.S. farming. *Rural Sociology, 69*(3), 370–385.

MacKinnon, D., and K. D. Derickson. (2013). From resilience to resourcefulness: A critique of resilience policy and activism. *Progress in Human Geography, 37*(2), 253–270.

Maine Legislative Statutes. (2014). Retrieved November 10, 2014, from http://legislature .maine.gov/legis/statutes/.

Malinowski, Bronislaw. (1922). *Argonauts of the western Pacific.* London: G. Routledge and Sons.

Martin, D. G., and B. Miller. (2003). Space and contentious politics. *Mobilization: An International Quarterly, 8*(2), 143–156.

Marx, K. (1977) *Capital* (Vol. 1). (Ben Fowkes, Trans.). New York: Vintage. (Original work published 1867.)

Mascarenhas, M., and L. Busch. (2006). Seeds of change: Intellectual property rights, genetically modified soybeans and seed saving in the United States. *Sociologia ruralis, 46*(2), 122–138.

Massey, D. (2001). Talking of space-time. *Transactions of the Institute of British Geographers, 26*(2), 257–261.

Massey, D. (2005). *For space.* London: Sage.

Mata, Duarte. (2013). Link2greenway. Retrieved March 29, 2015, from http://link2green ways.blogspot.pt/2013/06/8-verdades-inconvenientes.html.

Mauss, M. (1954). *The gift: Forms and functions of exchange in archaic societies.* London: Cohen and West.

Mbembe, A. (2003). Necropolitics. *Public Culture, 15*(1), 11–40.

McCarthy, James, and Scott Prudham. (2004). Neoliberal nature and the nature of neoliberalism. *Geoforum, 35*(3), 275–283.

McDowell, L. (1999). *Gender, identity and place: Understanding feminist geographies.* Minneapolis: University of Minnesota Press.

McKittrick, K. (2006). *Demonic grounds: Black women and the cartographies of struggle.* Minneapolis: University of Minnesota Press.

McMichael, P. (2009). A food regime genealogy. *Journal of Peasant Studies, 36*(1), 139–169.

McMichael, P., and D. Myhre. (1991). Global regulation vs. the nation-state: Agro-food systems and the new politics of capital. *Capital and Class, 15*(1), 83–105.

Meyer, M. L. (1994). *The White Earth tragedy: Ethnicity and dispossession at a Minnesota Anishinabek reservation, 1889–1920*. Lincoln: University of Nebraska Press.

Miller, D. (1999). *Principles of social justice*. Cambridge, Mass.: Harvard University Press.

Molnar, T. J., P. C. Kahn, T. M. Ford, C. J. Funk, and C. R. Funk. (2013). Tree crops, a permanent agriculture: Concepts from the past for a sustainable future. *Resources, 2*(4), 457–488.

Morvaridi, B. (2012). Capitalist philanthropy and the new green revolution for food security. [Special issue, *Food security*]. *International Journal of Sociology of Agriculture and Food, 19*(2), 243–256.

Moss, P. (2002). *Feminist geography in practice: Research and methods*. Oxford: Blackwell.

MPR. (2011). Return to tradition on White Earth Reservation in fight against poverty, hunger. Minnesota Public Radio. Retrieved May 9, 2016, from http://www.mprnews.org/story/2011/10/04/poverty-hunger-white-earth.

Murdoch, J., and A. C. Pratt. (1993). Rural studies: Modernism, postmodernism and the "post-rural." *Journal of Rural Studies, 9*(4), 411–427.

Nagar, R. (2014). *Muddying the waters: Coauthoring feminisms across scholarship and activism*. Urbana: University of Illinois Press.

Nancy, J. (1991). *The inoperative community*. Minneapolis: University of Minnesota Press.

Neth, M. (1995). *Preserving the family farm: Women, community and the foundations of agribusiness in the Midwest, 1900–1940*. Baltimore: Johns Hopkins University Press.

Nyéléni. (2007). Proceedings of the Forum for Food Sovereignty held in Sélingué, Mali, February 23–27.

Nyers, P. (2006). *Rethinking refugees: Beyond states of emergency*. New York: Routledge.

Offer, A. (1997). Between the gift and the market: The economy of regard. *Economic History Review, 50*(3), 450–476.

Ong, A. (2007). *Neoliberalism as exception: Mutations in citizenship and sovereignty*. Chapel Hill: Duke University Press.

Ostrom, E. (1990). *Governing the commons: The evolution of institutions for collective action*. Cambridge: Cambridge University Press.

Otero, G. (2012). The neoliberal food regime in Latin America: State, agribusiness, transnational corporations, and biotechnology. *Canadian Journal of Development Studies/Revue canadienne d'études du développement, 33*(3), 282–294.

Patel, R. (2005). *Stuffed and starved: The hidden battle for the world food system*. Brooklyn: Melville.

Patel, R. (2009). What does food sovereignty look like? *Journal of Peasant Studies, 36*(3), 663–706.

Patel, R., and McMichael, P. (2009). A political economy of the food riot. *Review, 32*(1), 9–35.

Paxson, H. (2008). Post-pasteurian cultures: The microbiopolitics of raw-milk cheese in the United States. *Cultural Anthropology, 23*(1), 15–47.

Pennington, M. (2012). Elinor Ostrom, common-pool resources and the classical liberal tradition. In E. Ostrom, C. Chang, M. Pennington, and V. Tarko (Eds.), *The future of the commons: Beyond market failure and government regulation* (pp. 21–47). Institute of Economic Affairs Monographs. London: Institute of Economic Affairs.

Pimbert, M. P. (2008). *Towards food sovereignty: Reclaiming autonomous food systems.* London: International Institute for Environment and Development (IIED).

Pimbert, M. P. (2009). *Towards food sovereignty.* Gatekeeper 141. London: International Institute for Environment and Development.

Polanyi, K. (1944). *The great transformation: The political and economic origins of our time.* Boston: Beacon Press.

Poppendieck, J. (1999). *Sweet charity?: Emergency food and the end of entitlement.* New York: Penguin.

Proudhon, P. J. (1966). *What is property?: An enquiry into the principle of right and of government.* New York: H. Fertig. (Original work published 1890.)

Rabinow, P., and N. Rose. (2006). Biopowertoday. *BioSocieties 1,* 195–217.

Raman S., and R. Tutton. (2009). Life, science, and biopower. *Science, Technology and Human Values, 35*(5), 711–734.

Ray, J. (2012). *The seed underground: A growing revolution to save food.* White River Junction, Vt.: Chelsea Green.

Renard, M. C. (2003). Fair trade: Quality, market and conventions. *Journal of Rural Studies, 19*(1), 87–96.

Retberg, H. (2012). The new radical: Going back to our agricultural roots. Address given at Pennsylvania Women's Agricultural Network Conference, State College, Penn.

Rhoades, R. E., and V. D. Nazarea. (1999). Local management of biodiversity in traditional agroecosystems. In W. W. Collins and C. O. Qualset (Eds.), *Biodiversity in Agroecosystems* (pp. 215–236). Boca Raton, Fla.: CRC Press.

Rice, J. L. (2010). Climate, carbon, and territory: Greenhouse gas mitigation in Seattle, Washington. *Annals of the Association of American Geographers, 100*(4), 929–937.

Robinson, T. (2004). Hunger discipline and social parasites: The political economy of the living wage. *Urban Affairs Review, 40*(2), 246–268.

Rose, G. (1997). Situating knowledges: Positionality, reflexivities and other tactics. *Progress in Human Geography, 21*(3), 305–320.

Rose, N. (2007). *The politics of life itself.* Princeton, N.J.: Princeton University Press.

Rose, N., and C. Novas. (2004). Biological citizenship. In A. Ong and S. Collier (Eds.), *Blackwell companion to global anthropology* (pp. 439–463). Oxford: Blackwell.

Rosset, P. (2008). Food sovereignty and the contemporary food crisis. *Development, 51*(4), 460–463.

Roy, A. (2014). Slum-free cities of the Asian century: Postcolonial government and the project of inclusive growth. *Singapore Journal of Tropical Geography, 35*(1), 136–150.

Russell, E. J. (1966). *A history of agricultural science in Great Britain, 1620–1954.* London: Allen and Unwin.

Salatin, J. (2007). *Everything I want to do is illegal.* Swoop, Va.: Polyface.

Sauer, C. O. (1925). *The morphology of landscape.* Berkeley: University of California Press.

Schanbacher, W. D. (2010). *The politics of food: The global conflict between food security and food sovereignty.* Santa Barbara, Calif.: Praeger.

Schiavoni, C. (2009). The global struggle for food sovereignty: From Nyéléni to New York. *Journal of Peasant Studies, 36*(3), 682–689.

Schiller, B. (2013, June 11). Seattle's food forest open for foraging. *Fast Company*. Retrieved April 11, 2015, from http://www.fastcoexist.com/1682269/seattles-urban -food-forest-is-open-for-foraging.

Schmitt, C. (1922). *Political theology: Four chapters on the concept of sovereignty.* (George Schwab, Trans.). Chicago: University of Chicago Press.

Scott, J. C. (1998). *Seeing like a state: How certain schemes to improve the human condition have failed.* New Haven, Conn. Yale University Press.

Scott, J. C. (2008). *The art of not being governed: An anarchist history of upland Southeast Asia.* New Haven, Conn.: Yale University Press.

Selowsky, M. (1981). Income distribution, basic needs and trade-offs with growth: The case of semi-industrialized Latin American countries. *World Development, 9*(1), 73–92.

Semple, E. C. (1922). The influence of geographic conditions upon ancient Mediterranean stock-raising. *Annals of the Association of American Geographers, 12*(1), 3–38.

Sennett, R. (1992). *The fall of public man.* New York: W. W. Norton. (Original work published 1974.)

Shiva, V. (1991). *The violence of Green Revolution: Third world agriculture, ecology and politics.* Atlantic Highlands, N.J.: Zed Books.

Shiva, V. (2004). The future of food: Countering globalisation and recolonisation of Indian agriculture. *Futures, 36*(6), 715–732.

Shreveport Rate Cases, 234 U.S. 342, 34 S. Ct. 833, 58 L. Ed. 1341 (Supreme Court 1914).

Simpson, A. (2014). *Mohawk interruptus: Political life across the borders of settler states.* Durham, N.C.: Duke University Press.

Slocum, R. (2007). Whiteness, space and alternative food practice. *Geoforum, 38*(3), 520–533.

Slocum, R., J. Shannon, K. V. Cadieux, and M. Beckman. (2011). "Properly, with love, from scratch": Jamie Oliver's food revolution. *Radical History Review, 2011*(110), 178–191.

Smith, A. (1863). *An inquiry into the nature and causes of the wealth of nations.* Edinburgh: A. and C. Black.

Stammers, Neil. (1995). A critique of social approaches to human rights. *Human Rights Quarterly, 17*(3), 488–508.

Stammers, Neil. (1999). Social movements and the challenge to power. In M. Shaw (Ed.), *Politics and globalisations: Knowledge, Ethics and Agency.* London: Routledge.

State of Maine v. Brown, 95 A.3d 82, 2014 M.E. 79 (Me. 2014).

Storey, D. (2001). *Territory: The claiming of space.* Harlow, UK: Prentice Hall.

Strauss, A., and J. M. Corbin. (1990). *Basics of qualitative research: Grounded theory procedures and techniques.* Newbury Park, Calif.: Sage Publications.

Taylor, P. (2000). Sovereignty. In R. Johnston, D. Gregory, G. Pratt, and M. Watts (Eds.), *The dictionary of human geography* (pp. 766–767). Malden, Mass.: Blackwell.

Town of Sedgwick, Maine. (2011). Local food ordinance. Retrieved February 12, 2012, from www.sedgwickmaine.org/images/stories/local-food-ordinance.pdf.

Trauger, A. (2004) "Because they can do the work": Women farmers and sustainable agriculture. *Gender, Place and Culture, 11*(2), 289–307.

Trauger, A. (2007). Coming home to geography: A personal and intellectual journey across the disciplinary divides. In P. Moss and K. Falconer Al-Hindi (Eds.), *Feminisms in geography: Space, place and environment*, (pp. 84–91). Lanham, Md.: Rowman and Littlefield.

Trauger, A. (2014). Toward a political geography of food sovereignty: Transforming territory, exchange and power in the liberal sovereign state. *Journal of Peasant Studies, 41*(6), 1131–1152.

Trauger, A. (2015). Seed saving as satyagraha in Northern India? In A. Trauger (Ed.), *Food sovereignty in international context* (pp. 106–124). Routledge: London.

Trauger, A., and J. Fluri. (2014). Getting beyond the "God Trick": Toward service research. *Professional Geographer, 66*(1), 32–40.

Trauger, A., and A. Murphy. (2013). On the moral equivalence of global commodities: Placing the production and consumption of organic bananas. *International Journal of Sociology of Agriculture and Food, 20*(2), 197–217.

Trauger, A., and C. Passidomo. (2012). Towards a post-capitalist politics of food: Cultivating subjects of community economies. *ACME: An International E-Journal for Critical Geographies, 11*(2), 282–303.

Tyler, T. (1999). Social justice: Outcome and procedure. *International Journal of Psychology, 35,* 117–125.

UNFAO. (2013). World hunger facts. Retrieved October 22, 2013, from www.worldhunger.org/articles/Learn/world%20hunger%20facts%202002.htm.

USDA Economic Research Service. (2009). *Access to affordable and nutritious food— Measuring and understanding food deserts and their consequences: Report to Congress.* Administrative Publication No. (AP-036).

van der Ploeg, J. D. (2009). *The new peasantries: Struggles for autonomy and sustainability in an era of empire and globalization.* London: Routledge/Earthscan.

van der Ploeg, J. D. (2010). The peasantries of the twenty-first century: The commoditisation debate revisited. *Journal of Peasant Studies, 37*(1), 1–30.

van Dooren T. (2008). Inventing seed: The nature(s) of intellectual property in plants. *Environment and Planning D: Society and Space, 26*(4), 676–697.

Valentine, G. (2005). Geography and ethics: Moral geographies? Ethical commitment in research and teaching. *Progress in Human Geography, 29*(4), 483–487.

Varsanyi, M. W. (2005). The rise and fall (and rise?) of non-citizen voting: Immigration and the shifting scales of citizenship and suffrage in the United States. *Space and polity, 9*(2), 113–134.

Vennum, T. (1988). *Wild rice and the Ojibway people.* St. Paul: Minnesota Historical Society Press.

Watts, M. (2000). *Struggles over geography: Violence, freedom and development at the millennium.* Heidelberg, Germany: Department of Geography, University of Heidelberg.

White, R. J., and C. W. Williams. (2012). The pervasive nature of heterodox economic spaces at a time of neoliberal crisis: Towards a "postneoliberal" anarchist future. *Antipode, 44*(5), 1625–1644.

Williamson, O. E. (1981). The economics of organization: The transaction cost approach. *American Journal of Sociology, 87*(3), 548–577.

Winne, M. (2008). *Closing the food gap: Resetting the table in the land of plenty.* Boston: Beacon Press.

Winter, M. (2003). Embeddedness, the new food economy and defensive localism. *Journal of Rural Studies, 19*(1), 23–32.

Wittman, H. (2009). Reframing agrarian citizenship: Land, life and power in Brazil. *Journal of Rural Studies, 25*(1), 120–130.

Wittman, H. (2010). Reconnecting agriculture and the environment: Food sovereignty and the agrarian basis of ecological citizenship. In H. Wittman, A. A. Desmarais, and N. Wiebe (Eds.), *Food sovereignty: Reconnecting food, nature and community* (pp. 91–105). Halifax, N.S.: Fernwood.

Wittman, H., A. A. Desmarais, and N. Wiebe (Eds.). (2010). *Food sovereignty: Reconnecting rood, nature and community.* Halifax, N.S.: Fernwood.

Wolford, W. (2010). *This land is ours now: Social mobilization and the meanings of land in Brazil.* Durham, N.C.: Duke University Press.

World Food Program (2013). Hunger statistics. Retrieved October 22, 2013, from http://www.wfp.org/hunger/stats.

Yakini, Malik. (2013, September). Address at Food Sovereignty: A Critical Dialogue, Yale University. *YouTube.* Retrieved April 11, 2015, from https://www.youtube.com/watch?v=_LaMt9HVQFY.

Yeoman, B. (2013, January 16). Rebel towns. *Nation.* Retrieved March 4, 2015, from http://www.thenation.com/article/172266/rebel-towns.

Zimmerer, K. S. (2003). Geographies of seed networks for food plants (potato, ulluco) and approaches to agrobiodiversity conservation in the Andean countries. *Society and Natural Resources, 16*(7), 583–601.

Žižek, S. (2006). *The parallax view.* Cambridge, Mass.: MIT Press.

INDEX

accumulation, 79–81, 107, 110; of capital, 20, 31, 50, 63, 92, 101; by dispossession, 12–13, 105–6; neoliberalism and, 68–69, 95, 120–22

agrarian citizenship, 29, 72

agrarian question, 4

anarchism, 14, 38–40, 55, 94, 107–9, 115–16

Anishinabek, 11, 85–90, 95–98, 100

anticapitalism, 39, 42, 92, 95, 98

Athens, Ga., 8–10, 52, 110–13, 117–19, 122

autonomous food production, 9, 34–39, 102, 122

autonomy, 2–3, 11, 14, 28; anarchism and, 109–10, 118–19; corporations and, 70; individual, 21; Nyéléni definitions and, 24–25, 34, 36–38; political, 6, 23–24, 46, 122–24, 126; self-governance and, 43, 55–56, 63–65, 79, 92

baldio, 57

biopolitics, 18, 29, 34, 49; food sovereignty as, 3, 14, 119; state authority and, 55–56, 61–63

Brown, Dan, 64, 76, 79

capitalism, 38, 42–43, 94–96, 123, 126; agriculture and, 4, 14, 34, 66, 91; food sovereignty and, 50, 107–10; liberal state and, 18–21, 26, 28, 34; white supremacy and, 2. *See also* anticapitalism

ceremony, 95–98

cities, 72, 80, 128; Athens, Ga., 113–17; gardens and, 39, 44, 49–52, 111; Lisbon, 56–57, 59–63

citizenship, 45, 55, 64–65, 68–72, 78–81

collective rights, 13, 37–40, 79–81, 125, 127, 136n1 (chap. 1)

colonialism, 13, 36, 41, 100. *See also* settler colonialism

commerce clause, 67, 69–70, 80

commodification, 14, 30, 85–86, 90–92, 104, 109

commodity, 90–95, 109; commodity production, 19, 68, 99, 104, 112; food as, 6, 85–86; food sovereignty and, 125–26; seeds as, 106–7

commons, 26; definition of, 39, 41, 46; lakes as, 98–100; urban commons, 49–51, 53–59, 61–63

Community Environmental Legal Defense Fund (CELDF), 64, 72–73, 77, 81, 127

community garden, 29, 49–51, 56, 109, 113–14

corporations, 19, 28, 50, 119–26; food and, 1–6; food sovereignty and, 22–24, 30, 36; neoliberalism and, 42–43; organic agriculture and, 66–67; rights and, 70–75, 78–79; seeds and, 103–5, 107, 112. *See also* food regime

court cases, 70–71, 76–77, 90, 106

democracy, 26, 37, 72, 76, 119; anarchism and, 109; food sovereignty and, 14, 25, 43–44, 81, 126–29

Detroit Black Farmers Community Food Security Network, 2, 51

Dillon's Rule, 71, 73–74. *See also* home rule

dispossession, 36, 88, 107, 120

double movement, 21, 35, 68

enclosure, 45, 50, 88, 100, 104–5; acts, 18–19, 108, 117; of commons, 53–54, 120. *See also* privatization

episteme, 12, 25, 32–34, 50

exchange, 51, 68, 79, 85–86; alternative forms of, 54, 79, 124–27; food sovereignty and,

GEOGRAPHIES OF JUSTICE AND SOCIAL TRANSFORMATION

1. *Social Justice and the City*, rev. ed.
by David Harvey

2. *Begging as a Path to Progress: Indigenous Women and Children and the Struggle for Ecuador's Urban Spaces*
by Kate Swanson

3. *Making the San Fernando Valley: Rural Landscapes, Urban Development, and White Privilege*
by Laura R. Barraclough

4. *Company Towns in the Americas: Landscape, Power, and Working-Class Communities*
edited by Oliver J. Dinius and Angela Vergara

5. *Tremé: Race and Place in a New Orleans Neighborhood*
by Michael E. Crutcher Jr.

6. *Bloomberg's New York: Class and Governance in the Luxury City*
by Julian Brash

7. *Roppongi Crossing: The Demise of a Tokyo Nightclub District and the Reshaping of a Global City*
by Roman Adrian Cybriwsky

8. *Fitzgerald: Geography of a Revolution*
by William Bunge

9. *Accumulating Insecurity: Violence and Dispossession in the Making of Everyday Life*
edited by Shelley Feldman, Charles Geisler, and Gayatri A. Menon

10. *They Saved the Crops: Labor, Landscape, and the Struggle over Industrial Farming in Bracero-Era California*
by Don Mitchell

11. *Faith Based: Religious Neoliberalism and the Politics of Welfare in the United States*
by Jason Hackworth

CPSIA information can be obtained
at www.ICGtesting.com
Printed in the USA
LVOW11s1740110517

534172LV00001B/70/P